M000100179

Network Security Essentials
Study Guide and Workbook
Volume 1 Second Edition

Created by: Pete Herzog
Marta Barceló Jordan
Bob Monroe

HACKING IS LEARNING
www.hackerhighschool.org

Copyright 2017, ISECOM
All rights reserved.
ISBN-13: 978-0978520717

Table of Contents

WARNING

Hacking is a methodology for learning and as with any learning tool there are dangers. Some lessons, if abused, may result in injury. Some additional dangers may also exist where there is not enough research on possible effects of emanations from particular technologies. Students using these lessons should be supervised yet encouraged to learn, try, and do. However the authors or ISECOM cannot accept responsibility for how any information herein is abused.

ISECOM

Introduction to this Network Security and Hacking Study Guide

There are hundreds of books written on networking and each one stands on its own merits. This book was not written to compete with any of those other works. This book was written to speed up the learning process and cut through some of the fluff. Don't bother to read our book if you want to know the names of people who wrote a certain protocol or dates when specific networking milestones occurred. If you want to know which university designed a certain networking function or which company patented a widget, than you picked up the wrong book.

We wrote this manual for speed of learning and ease of information retention.

We are not teaching you to be cracker, rather we are teaching you to work on contemporary and future systems. If you want to be a mechanic, you have to learn how to dissemble an engine. To be a successful network security professional, you need to know the inner workings of your digital world. This world includes portable devices (BYOD), servers, network protocols, hardware, software, security frameworks, principles of trust, virtual machines and dozens of other items.

Flipping through the pages you will notice that this book is not your typical technical guide. We designed everything to keep the reader engaged; to keep you interested. You will find segments like **Feed Your Head**, which are focused on deeper aspects of a topic. There are exercises that aren't just multiple choice questions but require you to actually think through a problem or research to find them. This is not a Dummies guide. This is a Hackers guide; old school hacker style.

The lessons from HackerHighschool.org which this manual follows and expands on have been an enormous task on behalf of the nonprofit Institute for Security and Open Methodologies (ISECOM.org).

Our guiding philosophy is to encourage all people across the world to embrace technology for its uses but not to harm others. Information should be free to the extent that it doesn't infringe on personal privacy or global peace.

So You Want to Be a Hacker?

Pretend I'm doing some sort of introduction here with statistics from like the police and some big corporation about network security. Good, you just made the first step toward hacking- you imagined something. With a few tips you're ready to go!

Computer hacking isn't just for criminals and security professionals. It's about knowing how things work down to a protocol level and what's going in and out of them.

You may have read that hacking requires "the hacker mindset." It doesn't. Most of what is called hacking today just requires you look for some key areas to find a hole or vulnerability. That's not magic. It's not even talent. It's pretty much just looking. But you need to know how to look. There's no hood you can throw open and look at an engine. We're talking invisible waves in the air and invisible data running over cables. This book is about being able to see that stuff and making sense of it.

You know there's all these awesome network tools mentioned in here that let you check on protocols, configure routers, remotely configure systems and troubleshoot? Well hackers use these tools to locate all the networks, servers, wireless devices, and gadgets. Try it. Use them to take a look at the network traffic and see what's flying across the wire and in the air. Look for what's not encrypted. Look all day and all week and make sure you think about whether something should be happening at the hour it's happening. That's how you hack networks for security.

When you're all done scanning and watching, if you find anything-- from protocols to services to systems to devices to people you didn't know about then you have just found your first threats. In security, all the unknowns, unused, and superfluous anything are a problem. It needs to be controlled or else it has to go.

See if you want to learn to hack networks you need to know how to learn how to figure out how things work on a network. To do that you need to use network tools just like network administrators do. The same tools. So what you're learning here is what equipment there is and how to use it for you to be the network hacker you want to be. Because if you can't see what it looks like when it's working, you won't figure out how it works, and you'll never be able to hack it.

Essential Commands

Introduction to Commands

Whether you've seen "hacking" in the 1995 movie *Hackers* or Trinity hacking into a UNIX system in *The Matrix Reloaded*, when you picture a hacker they're working at the command line. For good reason.

> You can do very big, very powerful things in the command line interface (**CLI**). You don't have to be a master at the command line but you should be comfortable working with it.

Once you've mastered the basics of the CLI, you can start using these commands in text files (called **scripts**); it's the easiest programming ever.

We will discuss commands and basic tools for Windows, OSX and Linux operating systems. You'll need to know them for exercises in the following lessons. At the end of this lesson, you should be familiar with:

- General Windows, Linux and OSX commands

- Basic network commands and tools, including

```
ping
tracert/traceroute
netstat
ipconfig/ifconfig
route
```

Getting Started

Requirements

To complete this lesson you will need:

- A PC running Windows

- A PC running Linux

- Optionally a Mac running OSX

- Access to the Internet

Setup

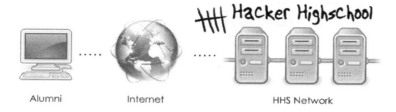

Figure 2.1: General Network Setup

This is the network in which we'll do most of our work. It consists of your PC, the Internet, and the ISECOM Hacker Highschool test network, which you will access through the Internet.

Note that access to the ISECOM test network is restricted. In order to gain access to it, your instructor must contact the system administrator, as detailed on the http://www.hackerhighschool.org web site.

However, you can also substitute any test network for these exercises. **NEVER** run tests against computers you don't own! That may be a criminal offense, and can be dangerous in lots of other ways.

If you want to set up your own test network, it can be as easy as testing another computer in your classroom or home. No special set-up is needed! Of course if you want something more robust or something that lets you experience the challenges and flaws of accessing another computer over the Internet, then you'll need an Internet-based test network. This can also be done by making alliances with other schools or homes and letting them access certain computers of yours remotely and you access theirs. But make sure you know what you're doing in setting it up because what you don't want is for those open computers to get hijacked by some random person on the Internet who does damage for which you will be responsible.

Operating System: Windows

In the days of yore, if we weren't working in UNIX, we all worked in DOS. We didn't need to open a CLI; we lived in one. Then UNIX developed "window" interfaces, an idea that eventually came to the PC with Microsoft Windows.

Once Windows arrived, we opened DOS in a window on our desktop and called that a **command prompt**. Long after Windows had moved beyond being DOS-based, Windows still has a CLI – and many people still call it a **DOS box**. It's not really DOS any more, but for our purposes, it doesn't matter. Here's how you open one.

How to open a CLI window

The procedure is similar for all versions of Windows.

1. Click the START button.

2. Choose the RUN option (skip this in Vista and later).

3. Type **command** if you are using Windows 95/98 or **cmd** for all other versions of Windows and press Enter or click OK.

4. A window similar to the following will appear:

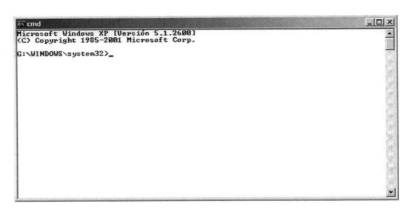

5. Now you can use the commands and tools listed below.

Commands and Tools (Windows/DOS)

Commands provide built-in operating system functions. Tools do more: they probe networks, search for **hosts** (which is, by the way, what we call computers attached to a network), and let you see or set your host's routing information.

Commands

Words in italics are options that you must enter.
Some commands have both long and short versions.

Command	Purpose
date	Display or set the date
time	Display or set the time
ver	Display the MS-DOS or Windows version
dir	Display the list of subdirectories and files in a directory.
cls	Clear the screen.
mkdir *directory* or md *directory*	Make a directory with the name *directory*: md tools
chdir *directory* or cd *directory*	Change the current directory to another directory: cd tools
rmdir *directory* or rd *directory*	Delete the directory: rd tools
tree *directory*	Display the structure of folders and files in text-graphic format: tree c:\tools
chkdsk	Check a disk and show a status report.
mem	Show the amount of memory used and free in the system.
rename *source dest* or ren *source dest*	Change the name of files: ren pictures MyPics

Command	Purpose
copy *source dest*	Copy one or more files to another location: `copy c:\tools\myfile.txt c:\tmp\`
move *source dest*	Move files and change the name of files and directories: `move c:\tools c:\tmp`
type *file*	Display the content of one or more text files: `type c:\tools\myfile.txt`
more *file*	Display the information screen by screen: `more c:\tools\myfile.txt`
delete *file* or **del** *file*	Delete one or more files: `del c:\tools\myfile.txt`

Tools

Words in italics are options that you must enter.

Tool	Purpose

ping *host*	Verify contact with the machine *host*.
	
	This command sends ICMP (Internet Control Message Protocol) ping packets to another computer to see how long it takes to respond, or if it responds at all. You can use a hostname or an IP address:
	
	`ping hackerhighschool.org`
	`ping 216.92.116.13`
	
	Options include:
	
	`ping -n 100 hackerhighschool.org`
	
	which sends 100 ping packets, and
	
	`ping -t 216.92.116.13`
	
	which pings the host until stopped with CTRL+C.
	
	To see more options:

Tool	Purpose
	`ping /h`

tracert *host*	Show the route that packets follow to reach the machine *host*.
	
	The DOS **tracert** command is an adaptation of the UNIX **traceroute**. (DOS commands could only be eight characters long, back in the day.) Both allow you to find the route that a packet follows from your host to the destination host, tracert also tracks how long each hop takes and travels, at the most, 30 hops. Often you can see the hostnames of the machines through which the packets travel:
	
	`tracert hackerhighschool.org`
	`tracert 216.92.116.13`
	
	Some options are:
	
	`tracert -n 25 hackerhighschool.org`
	
	to specify N, at the most, jumps, and
	
	`tracert -d 216.92.116.13`
	
	to hide hostnames.
	
	To see more options:
	
	`tracert /?`

ipconfig	Used alone, displays information on your host's active network interfaces (ethernet, ppp, etc.). It is similar to Linux **ifconfig**.
	
	Some options are:
	
	`ipconfig /all`
	
	to show more details
	
	`ipconfig /renew`
	
	to renew the network connection when automatic configuration with DHCP is used, and
	
	`ipconfig /release`
	
	to deactivate networking when DHCP is used.
	
	More options:

Tool	Purpose
	`ipconfig /?`

route print	Displays the routing table. **route** can also be used to set up or erase static routes.
	
	Some options:
	
	`route print`
	to show the list of routes,
	
	`route delete`
	to delete a route, and
	
	`route add`
	to add a route.
	
	More options:
	
	`route/?`

netstat	Displays information on the status of the network and established connections with remote machines.
	
	Some options:
	
	`netstat -a`
	to check all the connections and listening ports,
	
	`netstat -n`
	to display addresses and port numbers in numeric form, and
	
	`netstat -e`
	to sample Ethernet statistics.
	
	Options can be used together:
	
	`netstat -an`
	To see more options:
	
	`netstat/?`

For additional information on these commands and tools try these options:

```
command /h
command /?
help command
```

from a CLI window.

For example, for additional information on the tool **netstat**, you have three possibilities:

```
netstat /h
netstat /?
help netstat
```

Exercises

2.1 Open a CLI window and do the following:

a. Identify the exact version of DOS or Windows that you are using.

b. Identify the date and time of the system. If they are incorrect, correct them.

c. Identify all the directories and files that are in c:\.

d. Create the directory c:\hhs\lesson2. Copy to this directory the files with the extension .sys that are in c:\. What files have you found?

2.2 Identify the IP address of your host.

2.3 Trace the route to www.hackerhighschool.org. Identify IP addresses of the intermediate routers.

Game On: Taking Command

"Macrosoft Fenestra is neither an operating system nor an interface. It is a graphical system built around Solitaire," announced the technology teacher with bits of food stuck to the corners of his wet mouth. Mr. Tri was satisfied that the students bought that line of trash so he moved on. "Fenestra has a command interface, where you speak to the monitor and the computer does whatever it is that you want it to do. If you want a cup of coffee, just tell the monitor and a nice fresh cup of Joe appears."

Jace was so close to strangling this man, wondering if the police and judge would be sympathetic to her murder plea considering how he was butchering computer technology.

"Wait, hold on Mr. Tri." Jace hadn't let a breath out in the last ten minutes so her face was a funny color. "Sir, Fenestra is a graphical user interface, GUI, like the used gum you keep in that jar." Kids wrinkled their noses and giggled.

She got up and slid around him, getting behind the keyboard like a professional basketball player slipping past the defense. "Click Windows, type CMD, hit Enter. Check out the CLI. See that blinking line? That's where you type. See how it says what folder you're in?" Like a Formula 1 driver she never looked back; she just picked up speed.

"Now you can type CD C: and you're into the system root." Jace buried the throttle. "With a new system, you'll want to know as much as you can about your environment. Start by typing in VER, that's short for version. Now we can tell exactly what version of the operating system is running. See?" Students were staring. Mr. Tri was paralyzed.

Jace felt herself connecting with the computer, typing faster, becoming effortless. She mused out loud, "You can get a computer to spill its guts and tell you everything that's happening inside of it." Her fingers flew across the keyboard, dislodging a key and sending it into into the air where it landed in the moldy jar of old gum on the teacher's desk. Three girls in the front swallowed their gum.

Jace took this as her cue to stop. She stood up abruptly, giving the keyboard back to her teacher. His face was white and there was spit on his lips. She pulled a laser pointer from her inside jacket pocket quickly as if she were drawing a gun and shone it on Mr. Tri's forehead. A boy in the back of the class peed himself. Then turning it to the pathetic presentation slide on the screen at the front of the class, she calmly said,

"These slides are so wrong they have to go."

"Maybe it's you who should go," the teacher said, handing her a pass to the big man's office, the Vice Principal, aka the Principal of Vice. Her third pass this week. Technology was going to be the end of her, or at least the loss of her free time with another night of detention.

Game Over

Operating System: Linux

 Just like in Windows, when you're using Linux, you run commands in a CLI window. You'll see these called **consoles**, **terminals** and **shells**.

Feed Your Head: Console, Terminal or Shell?

Amaze your friends by knowing the difference.

- The **console** was actually the screen and keyboard attached directly to a computer back when the old people today used **dumb terminals** to access the computer remotely.

- You actually have your choice of **shell** in Linux, including **bash**, **tcsh** and **zsh**, among others. Different shells let you do very different things, and which one you like is almost a political issue. In most cases, you'll use bash. When you connect to the Hacker Highschool test network, you'll get an **empty shell**.

- When you open a **console window** what you're technically opening is a **terminal emulator** or **terminal window**, that is, a "fake" dumb terminal running in a window on your desktop.

What can you do at the Linux command line? Everything you could possibly do in any GUI tool, plus vastly more. Race your Windows friends to set your IP address: they will have to drill through all kinds of interfaces to do it. In Linux you could do it with:

```
ifconfig eth0 192.168.1.205
```

Bet you can type that faster than they can click!

How to open a terminal window

Because there are many versions of Linux, there are several ways to start a console window.

1. Click the Start Application button.

2. If you see a "Run Command" option, click it and enter "konsole", then Return.

3. Or look for Accessories, then choose Terminal.

4. Or on many systems you can press CTL-ALT-T.

5. A window similar to this will appear.

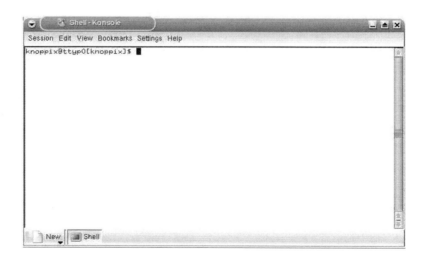

6. Now you can use the commands and tools listed below.

Linux Commands and Tools

Commands

Words in italics are options that you must enter.

Command	Purpose
date	Display or set the date.
time	Display or set the time.
fsck	Check a file system and show a status report.
cat *file*	Display the content of one or more text files: `cat /etc/passwd`
pwd	Display the name of the current directory.
hostname	Display the name of the computer you are currently using.
finger *user*	Display information on a user: `finger root`

ls	List the contents of the current directory:
	
	`ls -la`
	
	List the contents of another directory:
	
	`ls -la /etc`

cd *directory*	Change from current directory to *directory*. If no directory name is specified it changes to the home directory.
	
	For the login name "fred" the command
	
	`$cd`
	
	changes the directory to /home/fred, and
	
	`$cd -`
	
	changes to the last visited directory (think of "subtracting" one directory), and
	
	`$cd /tmp`
	
	changes to the /tmp directory.

cp *source dest*	Copy the file *source* to the file *dest*. Example:

Command	Purpose
	`cp /etc/passwd /tmp/bunnies`
rm *file*	Delete files. Only users with proper access permissions (or root) can delete specific files. `rm letter.txt`
mv *source dest*	Move or rename files and directories. Example: `mv secrets.zip innocent.zip`
mkdir *directory*	Make a directory with the name *directory*. Example: `mkdir tools`
rmdir *directory*	Delete the directory with the name directory but only if it is empty: `rmdir tools` Bonus question: how do you delete a directory with files in it?
find / -name *file*	Look for files, starting at /, with the name *file*: `find / -name myfile`
echo *string*	Write *string* to the screen: `echo hello`
command **>** *file*	**Redirect** the normal screen output of *command* to *file*: `ls > listing.txt` If this file already exist, it will get **clobbered**, meaning overwritten!
command **>>** *file*	Redirect the normal screen output of *command* to *file*. If the file already exists, it **appends** the output to the end of the file. Example: `ls >> listing.txt`

Command	Purpose
man *command*	Show the pages of the online manual about *command*: `man ls`

For additional information on these commands and tools try these options:

```
command -h
command --help
man command
help command
info command
```

For example, for additional information on the *ls* command, type in either of these two possibilities:

```
ls --help
man ls
```

Tools

Words in italics are options that you must enter.

Tool	Purpose
ping *host*	Verify the contact with the machine *host*: `ping www.google.com`
traceroute *host*	Show the route that the packets follow to reach the machine *host*: `tracert www.google.com`
ifconfig	Display information on active network interfaces (ethernet, ppp, etc.).
route	Display the routing table.
netstat	Display information on your network connections. `netstat -an`

Exercises

2.4   Identify the owner of the file **passwd**. (Note: first locate where this file is.)

2.5   Create the directory **work** in your own home directory (for example, if your login is **fred**, create the directory in /home/fred), and copy the file passwd to the directory work that you just created. Identify the owner of the passwd copy.

2.6   Create the directory **.hide** in the work directory (notice that the file name begins with a dot). List the contents of this directory. What did you have to do to see the contents of directory .hide?

2.7   Create the file **test1** with the content, "This is the content of the file test1" in the work directory. Create the file test2 with the content, "This is the content of the file test2" in the work directory. Copy into a file with the name **test** the contents of both previous files.

 Game On: Command Switches

At sixteen, Jace sometimes forgot to breathe when she was living on data. Maybe that was better now that the air smelled like burned coffee. The Vice Principal, Mr. McGurky, fixed her with an impatient stare while she pleaded with him. "But command line switches are the best part of the operating system!" Espresso brown hair drooped across the right side of her face. She lowered her head as if she were going to tackle the monitor at his desk. He didn't move out of her way yet somehow there she was already on his keyboard and challenging his computer to give up its command line secrets.

"See here's where we can find out which commands are available and what they do. We can either type in help or the command followed by help to see the switches and what they do. Check it out: we can stack a bunch of switches on a single command separated by a forward slash." Jace was speaking directly to the screen.

One of the secretaries was calling the local police department, thinking that this girl, this hacker, was going to infect them all with a virus. But the police just laughed when she explained the situation to them. The police officer said, "Jace, yeah we know Jace. She's a good kid and really knows her computer stuff. Nothing to be afraid of." But he could tell the confused secretary wasn't so convinced. "She was here last month helping us set up our network. Just tell 'er Officer Hank says to take a break because she's doing it again. She knows what I mean from last time when I had come out to calm down a bunch of librarians after she got in a fight with the technology desk over whether TCP port zero is a valid port or not."

The secretary didn't feel warm and fuzzy as she hung up. She was still not too sure about what this girl was doing on their computers. And the last thing she wanted was another virus taking down her Internet. So trying not to draw too much attention to herself, shaking like a little kid after a night of Trick or Treat feasting, she walked over to the power strip next to Mr. McGurky's file cabinets and stepped on the red lighted switch shutting down the computer system, the printer, the shredder, the coffee pot, and the coffee mug warmer. Jace froze as the screen went blank. She realized she'd done it again. Then she remembered to take a breath. But it was too late. Mr. McGurky was already writing her name across a week of detention slips.

Game Over

Operating System: OSX

Just like in Linux, when you're using OSX, you run commands in a CLI window. In OSX this application is called **Terminal**.

OSX is based on NetBSD and FreeBSD UNIX, ancestors of Linux. Its GUI and CLI approach is similar to Linux: you can do everything you could possibly do in any GUI tool, plus vastly more.

Some people think Windows stole the whole idea of a GUI from Mac. Actually, GUI interfaces and mouse pointers were used in a much older OS. You can know more than practically everybody by finding out which.

How to open a Terminal window

1. Click on the **Spotlight** icon, an icon of a magnifying glass typically located on the top right of your screen, and search for **Terminal**.

2. Then press Enter or click on it. You will see the Terminal window.

Typically Terminal is located under **Applications > Utilities**. Impress your friends by changing the Terminal style depending on your preferences. Press both the Command and comma keys to get the Preference dialog for Terminal and choose your preferred colors. Usually this keyboard shortcut gives you access to program preferences in OSX.

Commands and Tools (OSX)

Mac ships with a bash shell, so almost all typical Linux commands work on OSX as well.

Commands

Words in italics are options that you must enter.

Command	Purpose
`date`	Display or set the date.
`time` *`command`*	Display how long it takes for *command* to execute.
`fsck`	Check a file system and show a status report. If you use an OSX journaled volume such as Mac OSX 10.3 or later, in which journaling is enabled by default, you probably won't need to run this command.
`cat` *`file`*	Display the content of one or more text files: `cat /etc/passwd`
`pwd`	Display the name of the current directory.
`hostname`	Display the name of the computer you are currently using.
`finger` *`user`*	Display information on a user: `finger root`
`ls`	List the contents of the current directory:

Command	Purpose

	```ls -la```
	List the contents of another directory:
	```ls -la /etc```

cd *directory*	Change from current directory to *directory*. If no directory name is specified it changes to the user's home directory.
	For the login name "fred" the command
	```cd```
	changes the directory to /Users/fred, and
	```cd -```
	changes to the last visited directory (think of "subtracting" one directory), and
	```cd /tmp```
	changes to the /tmp directory.

cp *source dest*	Copy the file *source* to the file *dest*. ```cp /etc/passwd /tmp/bunnies```
rm *file*	Delete files. Only users with proper access permissions (or root) can delete certain files. ```rm letter.txt```
mv *source dest*	Move or rename files and directories. ```mv secrets.zip innocent.zip```
mkdir *directory*	Make a directory with the name *directory*. ```mkdir tools```
rmdir *directory*	Delete the directory with the name directory but only if it is empty: ```rmdir tools``` Bonus question: how do you delete a directory with files in it?

Command	Purpose
find / -name *file*	Look for files, starting at /, with the name *file*: `find / -name myfile`
echo *string*	Write *string* to the screen: `echo hello`
command > file	**Redirect** the normal screen output of *command* to *file*: `ls > listing.txt` If this file already exist, it will get **clobbered**, meaning overwritten!
command >> file	Redirect the normal screen output of *command* to *file*. If the file already exists, it **appends** the output to the end of the file. Example: `ls >> listing.txt`
man *command*	Show the pages of the online manual about *command*: `man ls`

For additional information on these commands and tools try these options:

```
command -h
command --help
man command
help command
info command
```

For example, for additional information on the *ls* command, type in either of these two possibilities:

```
ls --help
man ls
```

Tools

Words in italics are options that you must enter.

Tool	Purpose

`ping` *host*	Verify contact with the machine *host*.
	
	This command sends ping packets using ICMP (Internet Control Message Protocol) to another computer to see how long it takes to respond, or if it responds at all. You can use a hostname or an IP address:
	
	`ping www.hackerhighschool.org`
	`ping 216.92.116.13`
	
	Options include:
	
	`ping -c 100 www.hackerhighschool.org`
	
	which sends 100 ping packets, and
	
	`ping -t 216.92.116.13`
	
	which pings the host until stopped with CTRL+C.
	
	More options:
	
	`man ping`

`traceroute` *host*	Show the route that packets follow to reach the machine *host*.
	
	traceroute has the same scope as Windows **tracert** but uses different network protocols: traceroute uses UDP (User Datagram Protocol) and tracert uses ICMP (Internet Control Message Protocol). You may obtain different results using tracert and traceroute from same network source and destination.
	
	Both allow you to find the route that a packet follows from your host to the destination host. Each also tracks how long each hop takes and travels for, at the most, 30 hops. Often you can see the hostnames of the machines through which the packets travel:
	
	`traceroute www.hackerhighschool.org`
	`traceroute 216.92.116.13`
	
	To specify the maximum (-m) number of hops:

Tool	Purpose

	`traceroute -m 25 www.hackerhighschool.org`
	
	To save DNS lookups by showing the IP address rather than a hostname:
	
	`traceroute -n 216.92.116.13`
	
	To see more options:
	
	`man traceroute`

`ifconfig`	Used alone, displays information on your host's active network interfaces (ethernet, ppp, etc.). It is similar to Windows **ipconfig**.
	
	To show more details, meaning to be **verbose**:
	
	`ifconfig -v`
	
	To show only the *en1* network interface information:
	
	`ipconfig en1`
	
	To deactivate the network interface:
	
	`ifconfig en1 down`
	
	To bring it up:
	
	`ifconfig en1 up`
	
	Note: you must have permission to use this command, so you may need to put **sudo** in front of these commands. Then you will have to enter your password. **Use sudo carefully!**
	
	`sudo ifconfig en1 up`
	
	More options:
	
	`man ifconfig`

`netstat`	Displays information on the status of the network and established connections with remote machines. On BSD-like systems, **netstat** is also used to see your routing table. To sample all the connections and listening ports: `netstat -a`

Tool	Purpose

	To display the routing table:
	
	    `netstat -r`
	
	Used with -n to show addresses numerically:
	
	    `netstat -nr`
	
	To show information for *en1* network interface.
	
	    `netstat -r -ii en1`
	
	To see more options:
	
	    `man netstat`

Exercises

2.8 Identify the name and the IP address of your machine.

2.9 Trace the route to www.hackerhighschool.org. Identify IP addresses of the intermediate routers and find your path.

2.10 In Windows use **tracert** to see the path between you and www.hackerhighscool.org as see by Windows, and send the output on a file named **output.txt** for further analysis.

2.11 Then run the equivalent traceroute command on OSX and Linux from the same network, putting the output in files named **output2OSX.txt** and **output2Linux.txt**. Look at the output files carefully.

a. Are the paths the same or are there differences?

b. Did you find any lines containing the string:

    * * *

c. What does it mean?

d. Repeat this test at least an hour later. Are the results always the same?

Feed Your Head: Looking into Source Code

Want to know a command's every secret? Analyze its source code. One of big benefits of open source is that you can look into source code and, depending on license, also fork or edit it. So let's look at the source code for **nmap** – probably the world's most famous port scanner – to see it works. We chose this program on purpose: nmap code is particularly well commented.

We can access the source code at:

https://svn.nmap.org/nmap/

A good place to start digging into C/C++ code is looking for the **main()** function. So we look first at main.cc:

https://svn.nmap.org/nmap/main.cc

In C/C++ source code, multiline comments are wrapped in the character **/*** and ***/**, while `//` marks inline comments. Comments often contain "secret" information and pointers to other source code.

```
* * * * * * * * * * * * * * * * * * * * * * * * * * * * * * * * * * * * * * * * * * * * * * * * * * * * * * * * *
* * * * *
* main.cc -- Contains the main() function of Nmap. Note that
main() *
* does very little except for calling nmap_main() (which is in
nmap.cc) *
```

So we've found the main() function, but the "real" main is **nmap_main()** located in nmap.cc.

However we can also find preprocessor directives such as **#include** to "add" the

---

24

contents of another file to this one, and **#ifdef**, **#ifndef**, **#if**, **#endif**, **#else**, **#elif** for conditional inclusions.

When we search the file for main() we find:

```
int main(int argc, char *argv[]) {
  /* The "real" main is nmap_main(). This function hijacks
control at the beginning to do the following:
  3) Check the environment variable NMAP_ARGS.
  2) Check if Nmap was called with --resume.
  3) Resume a previous scan or just call nmap_main.
  */
```

So next we go to nmap.cc at

https://svn.nmap.org/nmap/nmap.cc

and search for nmap_main() to find:

```
int nmap_main(int argc, char *argv[]) {
  int i;
  std::vector<Target *> Targets;
  time_t now;
  struct hostent *target = NULL;
  time_t timep;
  char mytime[128];
addrset exclude_group;
```

Now we're in the right place to search for secret parameters accepted by nmap and hidden instructions for how it is used.

Exercise

One interesting issue is the format in which you can pass parameters to nmap.

Search for /* Convert a string like, then read the comments and source code to find the ways you can pass the port list to nmap.

Basic Command Equivalences for Windows, OSX and Linux

Words in italics are options that you must enter.

Linux	OSX	Windows
command --help	command --help	*command* /h, *command* /?
man *command*	man *command*	help *command*
cp	cp	copy
rm	rm	del
mv	mv	move
mv	mv	ren
more, less, cat	more, less, cat	type
lpr	lpr	print
rm -R	rm -R	deltree
ls	ls	dir
cd	cd	cd
mkdir	mkdir	md
rmdir	rmdir	rd
netstat -r	netstat -r	route print
traceroute	traceroute	tracert
ping	ping	ping
ifconfig	ifconfig	ipconfig

Beneath the Internet

Introduction and Objectives

In the far depths of the past, before there was an Internet, electronic communication was pure voodoo. Every computer manufacturer had their own idea about how machines should talk over a wire. And nobody even considered the possibility that a Wang computer might communicate with a Burroughs machine.

The world changed when scientists and students experienced the joy of using a terminal to access a mainframe computer. The famous IBM PC arrived, and quickly owners wanted to access that mainframe from their personal computer. Soon modems were making dial-up connections and users were working in terminal emulators. Networking had graduated to a Black Art, and the insiders were called (really) **gurus**.

The world shifted again dramatically when the Internet, which started as a military project, was opened to the public. Networking had always been local, meaning confined to one office or at most one campus. How were all these different systems going to talk?

The answer was "wedge" a universal address system into existing networks, a system we generally call **Internet Protocol (IP)**. Think about it this way: imagine your friend overseas sends you a package. That package may travel by plane, train or automobile, but you don't really need to know the airline schedule or the location of the nearest train station. Your package will eventually arrive at your street address, which is ultimately the only thing that matters. Your **IP address** is a lot like this: packets may travel as electrons, beams of light or radio waves, but those systems don't matter to you. All that matters is your IP address, and the IP address of the system with which you're talking.

One thing that complicates this idea in the real world is that more than one person may be living at a single address. In the networking world, that's what's happening when one server provides for instance both regular HTTP and secure HTTPS, as well as FTP. Notice the P at or near the end of those acronyms? That's always a dead giveaway for **protocol,** which is just another way of saying "a type of communication."

This lesson will help you understand how protocols and their ports work in Windows, Linux, and OSX. You'll also become familiar with several utilities (some of which have already been introduced in the previous lesson) that explore your system's networking capabilities.

At the end of the lesson you should have a basic knowledge of:

- the concepts of networks and how communication takes place
- IP addresses

- ports and protocols

Basic Concepts of Networking

The starting point for networking is the local area network (**LAN**). LANs let computers in a common physical location share resources like printers and drive space, and **administrators** control that access. Sections below describe common network devices and topologies.

Devices

Going forward in your career as a hacker, you're going to see a lot of network diagrams. It's useful to recognize the most common symbols:

| PC or Workstation | Hub | Switch | Router |

Figure 3.1: Common Network Symbols

A **hub** is like an old-fashioned telephone party line: everybody is on the same wire, and can hear everyone else's conversations. This can make a LAN noisy fast.

A **switch** is better: it filters traffic so that only the two computers talking to each other can hear the conversation. But like a hub, it's used only on a LAN.

A **router** sits between LANs; it's used to access other networks and the Internet, and it uses IP addresses. It looks at the packets being sent and decides which network those packets belong on. If the packet belongs on the "other" network, like a traffic police, it sends the packet where it belongs.

Topologies

A **topology** is just another way of saying "the way we connect it". The kind of decisions we make regarding our topology can affect positively as well as negatively in the future, depending on technologies being used, technological and physical constraints, performance and security requirements, size and nature of the organization, etc.

A LAN's physical structure can look like any of the following physical topologies:

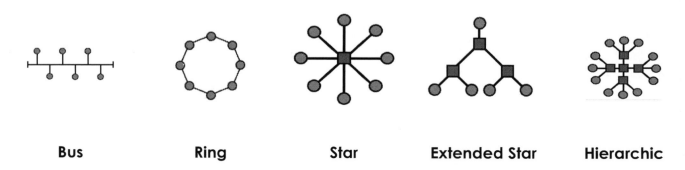

| Bus | Ring | Star | Extended Star | Hierarchic |

Figure 3.2: Toplogies

In a **bus** topology, all the computers are connected to a single cable, and each computer can communicate directly with any of the others. But break any part of the bus, and everyone's off the network.

In the **ring** configuration, each computer is connected to the following one, and the last one to the first, and each computer can only communicate directly with the two adjacent computers.

Bus topologies are rarely used nowadays. Ring technologies are often used at the inter-state level, usually with two counter rotating rings, sending traffic in opposite directions, for reliability and fault tolerance.

In the **star** topology, none of the computers are directly connected with others. Instead they are connected through a hub or switch that relays information from computer to computer.

If several hubs or switches are connected to each other, you get an **extended star** topology.

In a star or extended star topology, all the central points are **peers,** that is, they're essentially equals. This is the most common LAN topology today.

However, if you connect two star or extended star networks together using a central point that controls or limits traffic between the two networks, then you have a **hierarchical** network topology. This is the topology usually deployed in bigger enterprises.

Game On: Leaving the Back Door Open

In the sun-baked heat of the summer, Jace was happy to help the local air-conditioned police department set up their small network. They paid her with cookies, time away from the heat, conversation and the opportunity to install backdoors. Crawling under steel work desks that hadn't been moved in decades, Jace had found the cruddiest hidden spot to hide a wifi access point. She'd just plugged it in and sprinkled trash on top of it, and was dragging a roll of Ethernet cable to the wall ports she'd installed earlier.

A heavy hand slapped the desk above her. Jace kicked metal and yelled "Ow! My head!" then added, "you sure you don't want me to set up your server?"

The cop cleared his throat and tried to put on a Dork Professor voice. "Well I would, but I'm not sure how the flux ray resistor would hold up to the micro-channel cross feeds. Especially when the full moon falls on the last Tuesday of the month."

Jace flapped her feet in mock teen irritation. "Apparently you have no problem achieving quantum levels of baloney. And when do I get my cookies, Officer Kickam?"

"Jace please, please call me Hank. You make me feel like an old man when you call me Officer Kickam." He tried to sound hurt but she knew social engineering when she heard it: he was really trying to distract her from the cookies.

"Hank, hate to break the news to you, but you *are* an old man."

"Ouch, that hurt. I am not old, I am distinguished," he countered, considering his highly polished black police shoes as Jace's tattered sneaks disappeared under the heavy desk. Then cinnamon brown eyes and a face covered in spider webs emerged. Jace still had a reel of cable under one arm. Hank helped her up and brushed the bug webs off her face and shoulders.

"Help, police brutality," Jace teased.

"Hostile criminal," Hank returned. "So educate me on your diabolical plan here," the hairy muscled lawman asked in what almost sounded to Jace like a pleading tone.

That felt good, so she asked, "Are you sure you want to know about this networking stuff?" He nodded eagerly. Jace thought: *bobble head*.

"Okay, what I did was design a network topography, like a map that shows where all the equipment, computers, hubs, jacks, switches, routers and firewalls will go. You can't start a project like this without a map," she said, glancing up at the cop. "It's all about making sure every node can talk to every other node, with no single point of failure. So, like, a bus architecture stinks, because if one node in the bus goes down, everyone else does too." Hank nodded so Jace continued.

"Think like networking is this cop shop, uh, police station, and someone just brought in a suspect. Every cop deserves their fair turn to beat up on the guy without hogging someone else's time. If the victim, I mean suspect, is moved to another cell, all the cops who still need to beat on the dude have to know where he went."

"Oh Jace, you're gonna start looking like you need a good beating too if you keep talking like that about us peace officers." Hank pulled up his gun belt and sucked in his slight belly.

Jace snorted a laugh. "So the suspect is a data packet and you police thugs are the network devices. And every device, a switch, a router, firewall, another server or whatever, needs to know that the data packet gets dealt with. You know, pummeled with police batons. I think you called it giving someone a wood shampoo."

Hank rolled his eyes and groped for the baton that he didn't have on him.

Giggling, Jace brought up the reel of cable like a shield. "Hey, I've got a spool of wire and I'm not afraid to use it. Put down the cup of coffee and nobody gets hurt." Off balance and laughing, Jace flopped onto Hank, who didn't budge. *Wow, this guy is a total rock*, she realized. The hand he laid on her shoulder reminded her of … something.

She stood a little too quickly, reddening. "So there's two kinds of devices. Smart devices and dumb ones. Just like cops." Four approaching uniforms appeared at exactly the wrong time to hear the "dumb ones, just like cops." Lamely Jace continued, "Smart devices remember everything they do. They keep logs of their activities."

"And the dumb ones? Like cops?" asked the Chief of Police.

Game Over

The TCP/IP (DoD) Model

TCP/IP was developed by the **DoD (Department of Defense)** of the United States and **DARPA (Defense Advanced Research Project Agency)** in the 1970s. TCP/IP was designed to be an open standard that anyone could use to connect computers together and exchange information between them. Ultimately, it became the basis for the Internet.

Generally, the simplest form of the TCP/IP model is called the **DoD Model**, and that's where we'll start.

Layers

The simple DoD model defines four totally independent layers into which it divides the process of communication between two devices. The layers that pass information are:

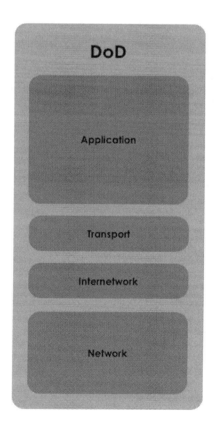

Figure 3.3: The DoD Model

Application

The application layer is exactly what you probably think it is: the layer where applications like Firefox, Opera, email clients, social networking sites, instant messaging and chat applications work. Actually quite a few applications access the Internet: some office applications, for instance, connect to online collections of clip art. The application layer creates the payload that all the other layers carry. A good analogy is a postal system. The application creates the package that it wraps with instructions on how the package should be used. Then it hands off the package to the mail room: the Transport layer.

Transport

The transport layer sets up network connections, which are called **sessions.** In the world of the Internet, the primary protocol at the Transport layer is **TCP, the Transmission Control Protocol**. TCP adds another "wrapping" to the outside of the package, with instructions about which package it is (say, 1 of 3), how to make sure the package got there, and whether the package is intact.

Let's say you're going to email a letter to your mother. The letter may be tiny or huge, but it's too big to send over the Internet in one piece. Instead, TCP breaks up that letter into **segments,** small chunks that are consecutively numbered, with a little bit of error-checking code at the end. If a packet gets corrupted in transit, TCP requests a retransmission. At the receiving end, TCP puts the pieces back together in the correct order and your mother gets the letter in her email.

But don't forget that TCP isn't the only game in town: **UDP** also functions at this layer, and in particular it does NOT create sessions. It just shoots a stream of **datagrams**, which are similar to segments, but UDP never checks if you've received it.

Whether TCP or UDP, all traffic is assigned to specific **port numbers** at this layer.

Internetwork

This layer adds information about the source and destination addresses, and where the **packet** begins and ends. It's like a delivery company that gets packages to the correct address. It doesn't care if all the packets make it, or if they are intact; that's the Transport layer's job. The major protocol at this level is, appropriately, **IP (Internet Protocol)**. And this is the layer that uses IP addresses to get packets to the right place by the best route.

Network Access

This layer is the low-level physical network that you use to connect to the Internet. If you're dialing up, we're sorry, and you're using a simple **PPP** connection. If you have **DSL** you may be using **ATM** or **Metro Ethernet**. And if you have cable Internet you're using a **DOCSIS** physical network. It doesn't matter what kind you use, because TCP/IP makes everything work together. The network access layer consists of the Ethernet cable and **network interface card (NIC)**, or the wireless card and access point. It handles the lowest level ones and zeroes (bits) as they go from one point to another.

> ### Feed Your Head: See "The OSI Model"
>
> *See "The OSI Model" at the end of this lesson for an alternative take on network modeling.*

Protocols

So now you're connected to the Internet. That seems simple enough, but consider the usual situation you're in: you are conducting innocent, important research on the Internet, while your dear brother or sister is wasting time streaming a movie. Why don't these two streams of traffic get mixed up? How does the network tell them apart?

The answer is **protocols,** which are like languages that different kinds of traffic speaks. Web traffic uses one protocol, file transfers another one, and email a different one still. Like all things digital, protocols don't really use names down at the network level; they use IP addresses and **port numbers**.

Application layer protocols

FTP or *File Transfer Protocol* is used for the transmission of files between two devices. It uses one port to deliver data, and another port to send control signals ("I got the file! Thanks!"). The most commonly used ports are 20 and 21 (TCP).

HTTP or *Hyper-Text Transfer Protocol* is used for web pages. This traffic usually uses TCP port 80. **HTTPS** is a secure variant that encrypts network traffic, usually on TCP port 443.

SMTP or *Simple Mail Transfer Protocol* is the protocol that sends email. Its TCP port is 25.

DNS or *Domain Name Service* is how a domain like ISECOM.org gets mapped to an IP address like 216.92.116.13. It uses port is 53 (UDP).

Transport layer protocols

TCP and **UDP** are the two main protocols used by the transport layer to transfer data.

TCP or Transmission Control Protocol establishes a logical connection (a **session**) between two hosts on a network. It sets up this connection using the three-way handshake.

1. When my computer wants to connect with yours, it sends a **SYN** packet, which is basically saying, "Let's synchronize clocks so we can exchange traffic with timestamps."

2. Your computer (if it's going to accept the connection) responds with a **SYN/ACK** acknowledgment packet.

3. My computer seals the deal with an **ACK** packet, and we're connected.

But this happens only with TCP. Instead, **UDP or User Datagram Protocol** is a transport protocol that doesn't even care if you have a connection. It's like a fire hose: if you catch the stream you catch it, and if you don't, you don't. This makes UDP very fast, so it's useful for things like streaming voice and video, where missing a single frame doesn't matter much or online gaming, where missing a single frame doesn't matter much (depending on which side of the bullet you are).

Internet layer protocols

IP or Internet Protocol serves as a universal protocol to allow any two computers to communicate through any network at any time. It's like the postal carrier who delivers mail; all it does is get packets to their destination address.

Internet Control and Management Protocol (ICMP)

ICMP is the protocol that the network devices and network administrators use to troubleshoot and maintain the network. It includes things like **ping** (Packet InterNet Groper) and similar commands that test the network and report errors. Because people have used things like ping floods to bring down hosts and networks, most systems limit ICMP to one response per second.

To summarize, ports and protocols come together like this:

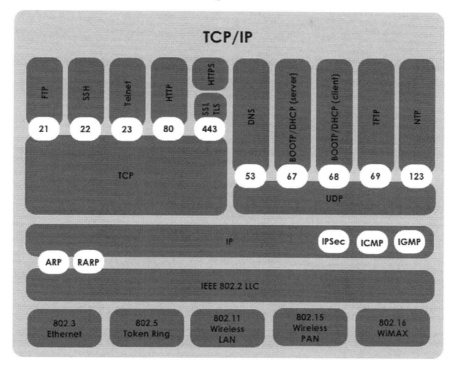

Figure 3.4: The TCP/IP Stack

IPv4 Addresses

Domain names are handy for humans, because we're good at remembering names like ISECOM.org. But networks don't actually understand them; they only understand numeric IP addresses. So when you ask for ISECOM.org, your computer does a quick lookup using **DNS (Domain Name Service)** to find the corresponding IP address.

IP addresses are like street addresses. If you want mail, you have to have one. **IPv4** addresses consist of 32 bits that are divided in four 8-bit **octets**, which are separated by dots. This means that there are 2^{32} (or 4,294,967,296) unique addresses on the Internet under IPv4. Part of the IP address identifies the network, and the remainder of the IP address identifies the individual computers on the network. Think of these parts as the country/city (network) portion of the address and the street (host) portion of the address.

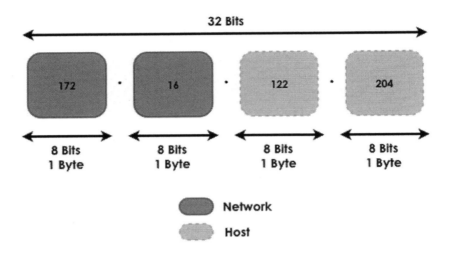

Figure 3.5: Network Number and Host ID

Returning to the postal service analogy: IP is the delivery truck that gets the packet to the correct post office. TCP is the outer wrapper with the list of how many packages are in a shipment, and which one this is (say, number 3 of 65). The host-level addresses are the particular house (computer) for which the packet is destined.

There are both public and **private (non-routable) IP addresses**. Private IP addresses are used by private networks; routers won't allow these addresses onto the Internet.

IP addresses within a private network should not be duplicated within that network, but computers on two different – but unconnected – private networks could have the same IP addresses. The IP addresses that are defined by IANA, the Internet Assigned Numbers Authority, as being available for private networks (see RFC 1918) are:

      10.0.0.0 through 10.255.255.255   (Class A)

      172.16.0.0 through 172.31.255.255   (Class B)

      192.168.0.0. through 192.168.255.255 (Class C)

Classes

IP addresses are divided into classes based on what portion of the address is used to identify the network and what portion is used to identify the individual computers.

Depending on the size assigned to each part, more devices will be allowed within the network, or more networks will be allowed. The existing classes are:

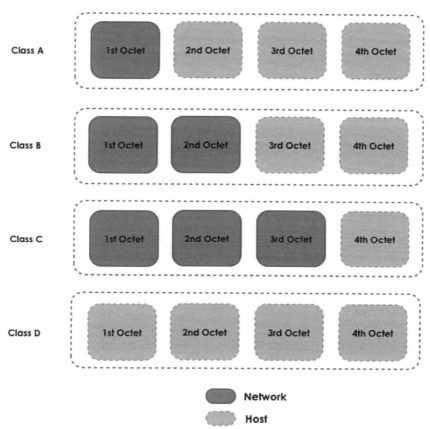

Figure 3.6: IP Class Divisions

Class A: The first bit is always zero, so this class includes the addresses between 0.0.0.0 (which, by convention, is never used) and 126.255.255.255. Note: the addresses of 127.x.x.x are reserved for the services of loopback or localhost (see below).

Class B: The first two bits of the first octet are '10', so this class includes the addresses between 128.0.0.0 and 191.255.255.255.

Class C: The first three bits of the first octet are '110', so this class includes the addresses between 192.0.0.0 and 223.255.255.255.

Class D: The first four bits of the first octet are '1110', so this class includes the addresses between 224.0.0.0 and 239.255.255.255. These addresses are reserved for group multicast implementations.

The remaining addresses are used for experimentation or for possible future allocations.

The **mask (or netmask)** is used to mark these class splits. Down in binary, a '1' bit shows the part containing the network identification and a '0' bit represents the part that identifies the individual host. The default netmasks for the first three classes are:

255.0.0.0   (Class A)

255.255.0.0   (Class B)

255.255.255.0   (Class C)

This is actually pretty slick, since networks that use default classes will mask one octet if they're Class A, two octets for Class B and three octets for Class C. Using default classes is handy – but not everyone's doing it.

What all this means is that to identify a host, you'll need both the IP address and a network mask:

```
IP: 172.16.1.20
Mask: 255.255.255.0
```

Loopback Addresses

IP addresses 127.0.0.1 through 127.255.255.254 are reserved to be used as **loopback** or localhost addresses, that is, they refer directly back to the local computer. Every computer has a localhost address of 127.0.0.1, therefore that address cannot be used to identify different devices.

There are also other addresses that cannot be used. These are the **network address** and the **broadcast address**.

Network Addresses

The network address is basically the network part of an IP address, **with zeroes where the host part would be**. This address cannot be given to a host, because it identifies the whole network, not just one host.

> IP: 172.16.1.**0**
>
> Mask: 255.255.255.0

Broadcast Addresses

The broadcast address is basically the network part of an IP address, **with ones where the host part would be**. This address can't be used to identify a specific host, because it's the address that all hosts listen to (of course that's what broadcast means: everybody listens).

> IP: 172.16.1.**255**
>
> Mask: 255.255.255.0

Feed Your Head: IPv6

ICANN/IANA assigned the final /8 IPv4 address blocks to the Regional Internet Registries in February 2011. That means we're officially out of IPv4 addresses.

IPv6 (Internet Protocol version 6) is a version of the Internet Protocol (IP) developed by the Internet Engineering Task Force (IETF) to succeed IPv4. To put it simply, it gives us more numbers by using a 128-bit address compared to the 32-bit addresses in IPv4.

IPv6 incorporates many different types of addresses, including unicast and multicast.

IPv6 Address Types

Type Of Address	Purpose	Prefix	Easily Seen Hex Prefix
Global Unicast	Unicast packets sent through the	2000::/3	2 or 3

Feed Your Head: IPv6

Type Of Address	Purpose	Prefix	Easily Seen Hex Prefix
	public Internet; only one host listens.		
Unique Local	These addresses are routed only within a set of cooperating sites. These were introduced in the IPv6 to replace the site-local addresses. These addresses also provide a 40-bit pseudorandom number that reduces the risk of address conflicts.	FD00::/8	FD
Link Local	This is a link-local prefix offered by IPv6. This address prefix signifies that the address is valid only in the local physical link.	FE80::/10	FE80
Multicast	Multicasts that stay on the local subnet; all hosts listen.	FF02::/16	FF02

Address Format

An IPv6 address is represented by 8 groups of 16-bit hexadecimal values separated by colons (:). For example:

    2001:0db8:85a3:0000:0000:8a2e:0370:7334

The hexadecimal digits are case-insensitive.

An IPv6 address can be abbreviated with the following rules:

1. Omit leading zeroes in a 16-bit value.

2. Replace one or more groups of consecutive zeroes by a double colon. For example:

Feed Your Head: IPv6

Address	fe80	: 0000	: 0000	: 0000	: 0202	: b3ff	: fe1e	: 8329
After Rule 1 fe80		: 0	: 0	: 0	: 202	: b3ff	: fe1e	: 8329
After Rule 2 fe80	:	:	:	: 202	: b3ff	: fe1e	: 8329

Here are the text representations of these addresses:

```
fe80:0000:0000:0000:0202:b3ff:fe1e:8329

fe80:0:0:0:202:b3ff:fe1e:8329

fe80::202:b3ff:fe1e:8329
```

Another interesting example is the loopback address:

```
0:0:0:0:0:0:0:1

::1
```

Dual IP Stack Implementation

Most modern computers can have both an IPv4 and an IPv6 address, so the host can send IPv4 packets to other IPv4 hosts and can send IPv6 packets to IPv6 hosts.

The dual stack approach is a reasonable approach to migrate to IPv6.

Tools

Linux: `ifconfig, ping6, traceroute6`

Windows: `ipconfig, ping, tracert`

Exercises

This works best if you have a partner.

3.1.   Check your IPV6 address. Can you swap it with your partner?

Feed Your Head: IPv6

> 3.2.   Ping your partner's IPv6 address. What response do you get?

Ports

Both TCP and UDP use **ports** to exchange information with applications. A port is an extension of an address, like adding an apartment or room number to a street address. A letter with a street address will arrive at the correct apartment building, but without the apartment number, it won't get to the correct recipient.

Ports work in the same way. A packet can be delivered to the correct IP address, but without the associated port, there is no way to determine which application should act on the packet. A port number is also a 16 bit number, which means it can have decimal values between 0 and 65535 (2 to the power of 16).

> Another way to think about this would be: every computer is a post office. Each application has its own post office box; no two applications should share the same post office box. The port number is that post office box number.

Port numbers make it possible to have multiple streams of information going to one IP address, where each one is sent to the appropriate application. The port number lets a service running on a remote computer know what type of information a local client is requesting and what protocol is used to send that information, all while maintaining simultaneous communication with a number of different clients.

For example, if a local computer attempts to connect to the website www.osstmm.org, whose IP address is 62.80.122.203, with a web server running on port 80, the local computer would connect to the remote computer using the **socket address**:

62.80.122.203:80

In order to maintain a level of standardization among the most commonly used ports, IANA has established that the ports numbered from 0 to 1024 are to be used for common, **privileged** or **well-known services.** The remaining ports – up through 65535 – are used for dynamic allocations or particular services.

The most commonly used (well-known) ports – as assigned by the **IANA** – are listed here:

Port Assignments		
Number	**Keywords**	**Description**
0		Reserved
1-4		Unassigned
5	rje	Remote Job Entry
7	echo	Echo
9	discard	Discard
11	systat	Active Users
13	daytime	Daytime
15	netstat	Who is Up or NETSTAT
17	qotd	Quote of the Day
19	chargen	Character Generator
20	ftp-data	File Transfer [Default Data]
21	ftp	File Transfer [Control]
22	ssh	SSH Remote Login Protocol
23	telnet	Telnet
25	smtp	Simple Mail Transfer

Port Assignments

37	time	Time
39	rlp	Resource Location Protocol
42	nameserver	Host Name Server
43	nicname	Who Is
53	domain	Domain Name Server
67	bootps	Bootstrap Protocol Server
68	bootpc	Bootstrap Protocol Client
69	tftp	Trivial File Transfer
70	gopher	Gopher
75		any private dial out service
77		any private RJE service
79	finger	Finger
80	www-http	World Wide Web HTTP
95	supdup	SUPDUP
101	hostname	NIC Host Name Server
102	iso-tsap	ISO-TSAP Class 0
110	pop3	Post Office Protocol - Version 3
113	auth	Authentication Service
117	uucp-path	UUCP Path Service
119	nntp	Network News Transfer Protocol

Port Assignments

123	ntp	Network Time Protocol
137	netbios-ns	NETBIOS Name Service
138	netbios-dgm	NETBIOS Datagram Service
139	netbios-ssn	NETBIOS Session Service
140-159		Unassigned
160-223		Reserved

Game On: You Got To Keep Them Separated

Jace sucked in her lower lip and tried to come up with a cop-oriented explanation Officer Hank would understand. "You don't keep everyone you arrest together, you separate them out, right?"

"Of course not, we put 'em all in the same pit. After a few days, we haul off whoever's left to see the judge." He gave her the look you save for people with three heads.

Jace hopped up on top of the sticky metal police desk. "Well, I'm hoping you don't put the litterbugs with the terrorists, do you? So you sort out the chainsaw Jasons from the traffic-light runners" Jace pretended not to notice as files of police reports slid off the desk.

Hank put on a fake frown and the classic cop pose, wagging his finger over her. "The pit, remember the pit."

"Oh yeah, it reduces paperwork," she grinned back, peeling carbon copies from her tush.

"Network traffic has to be separated the same way, but with less bloodshed. Data packets, and gang bangers, have to be routed from their original location to their destination. You can't let data escape like criminals," Jace laughed.

"Oh, you're a real comedian. Let me introduce you to our newest jailhouse guest,

Shawn the Lawn Strangler." Too late, Officer Hank wanted to bite back his words.

Jace's voice went flat. "Specific ports go with specific protocols. Ports zero through ten-twenty-three are special, just for servers. Port 80 is for HTTP to send HTML. You can redirect them with rules in your router. Like telnet uses port 23 but you can redirected it to any other port that's not in use." She had stopped blinking, holding firmly onto the image of beads of light sliding down copper wires.

Dang it, thought Hank. *Wrong direction!*

"Ports that aren't in use should be turned off or put in stealth mode. If a port gets pinged, it should never respond. Port scanning's a common tactic to see if any port on any IP address range is open and left unused. If a port responds to a port scan, an attacker can use that information to access vulnerabilities and introduce exploits into a network." She sounded like an answering machine.

Mouth narrowing, she continued, "a good port scan is conducted as a passive measure, instead of active. Otherwise the scan's going to trigger network alarms, or an intrusion detection system, the firewalls, behavioral tracking programs, audit logs, something. Can't have that...."

A clipboard fell off the desk to the tiled floor with a sound that shocked Jace back to the office. Lights sparkled inside her retinas as she sucked air hard.

Officer Hank was beside her, arm around her. "Hang on, Jace. Come on, drop that, let's get out of here and talk."

Game Over

Encapsulation

When a piece of information – an e-mail message, for example – is sent from one computer to another, it is subject to a series of transformations. The application layer generates the data, which is then sent to the transport layer.

The transport layer takes this information, breaks in into segments and adds a header to each one, which contains ports, unique number of the segment and other session information.

Then the segment is passed to Network layer where another header is added, containing the source and destination IP addresses and more meta-information.

The next layer, which in most local networks is supplied by Ethernet, adds yet another header, and so on. This procedure is known as **encapsulation.**

Each layer after the first makes its data an encapsulation of the previous layer's data, until you arrive at the final layer, in which the actual transmission of data occurs. So encapsulation looks like this:

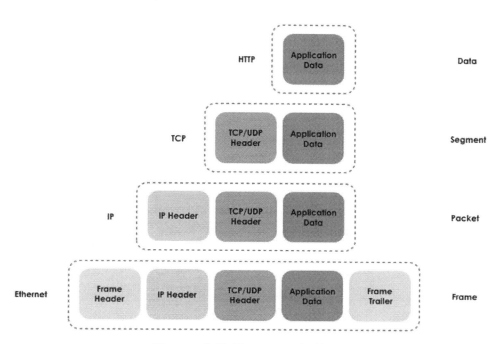

Figure 3.7: Encapsulation

When the encapsulated information arrives at its destination, it must then be de-encapsulated. As each layer passes information to the next layer up the stack, it removes the information contained in the header placed there by that lower layer.

The final bit of information in this great addressing scheme is the absolutely unique address of the computer's NIC: the **Media Access Controller (MAC) address**. This address is usually displayed as six two-character **hexadecimal** numbers separated by colons or hyphens (dashes). It is the physical address of the network card and supposedly can't be changed (actually, there are ways to change it, but exactly how is for you to figure out). A MAC address looks like this:

00-15-00-06-E6-BF

Exercises

3.1.   Using commands you learned in Lessons 1 and 2, get your IP address, netmask, DNS hostname, and MAC address. Compare these with your partners. What seems similar and what is different? Given the IP address scheme the network is using, is this a private or a public network?

3.2.   Netstat - The **netstat** command tells you your network statistics: with whom you're connected, how long networking has been up, and so forth. In Linux, Windows or OSX you can open a command line interface and type:

```
netstat
```

In the CLI window, you'll see a list of established connections. If you want to see the connections displayed in numeric form, type:

```
netstat -n
```

To see the connections and the active (listening, open) ports, type:

```
netstat -an
```

To see a list of other options, type:

```
netstat -h
```

In the netstat output, look for the columns listing the local and remote IP addresses and the ports they're using:

```
Proto Recv-Q Send-Q  Local Address      Foreign Address     (state)
tcp4    0        0  192.168.2.136.1043  66.220.149.94.443
ESTABLISHED
```

a. The ports are the numbers after the regular IP address; they may be separated by dots or colons. Why are the ports used by the remote address different from the ports used by the local address?

Open several browser windows or tabs to various websites, then run netstat again.

b. If there are several tabs open, how does the browser know which information goes to which tab?

c. Why is it that when a web browser is used, no listening port is specified?

d. What protocols are used?

e. What happens when one protocol gets used in more than one instance?

3.3.   My First Server

To perform this exercise, you must have the **netcat (nc)** program. BackTrack includes it by default, as does OSX, but you can download installers for various operating systems.

In a CLI window, type:

```
nc -h
```

This displays the options that are available in netcat.

To create a simple server, In Linux or Windows type:

```
nc -l -p 1234
```

or in OSX type:

```
nc -l 1234
```

You just started a server listening to port 1234.

Open a second CLI window and type:

```
netstat -a
```

This should verify that there is a new service listening on port 1234.

To communicate with a server, you have to have a client! In your second CLI window type:

```
nc localhost 1234
```

This command makes a connection with the server that's listening to port 1234. Now, anything that is written in either of the two open CLI windows can be seen in the other window.

a. Consider the implications. How could someone abuse this capability to exploit your machine?

b. Netcat sends all its traffic in the clear. Is there a secure alternative?

c. Stop your server by going back to the first CLI window and typing Control-C.

d. Now create a simple text file named *test* containing the text, "Welcome to my server!"

e. Once you've done that, look at the following command and translate it for the instructor: what does each part do? Then, in your first CLI window, type:

```
nc -l -p 1234 < test
```

From another CLI window, connect to the server by typing:

```
nc localhost 1234
```

When the client connects to the server, you should see the output of the file *test*.

f. What protocol has been used to connect with the server?

g. Does netcat allow you to change this? If so, how?

Feed Your Head: The OSI Model

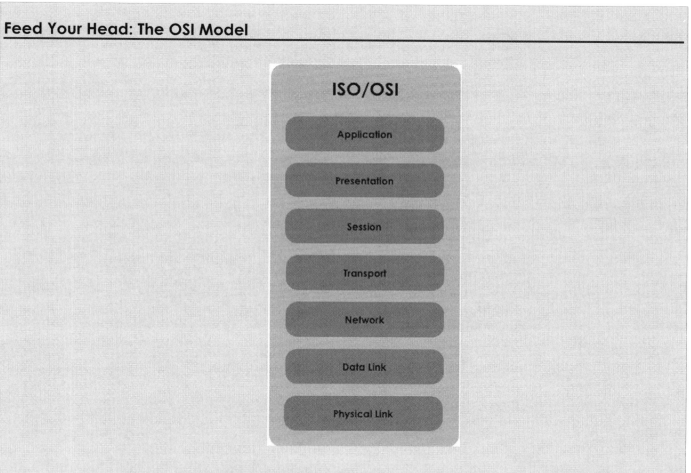

Figure 3.8: The ISO/OSI Model

The **OSI Model** was developed in the 1980s (about ten years after the TCP/IP Model) by **ISO**, the International Standards Organization. OSI stands for **Open Systems Interconnection**, and it was an attempt to standardize networking architecture that came from an organization that wasn't really involved in the development of networking.

The OSI Model is a layered model with a handful of simple rules. Similar functions are grouped together in the same layer, and (please do not forget this) every layer is serviced by the layer **beneath** it, and serves the layer **above** it.

This layered model is a good idea, because since every layer (in theory) does its own communication, new developments in any one layer don't break any of the other ones. This feature alone may explain the Internet boom we've had since 2000, with new applications and services appearing almost each day.

Besides the two rules of this OSI model we've already discussed (similar functions are grouped, and every layer is serviced by the layer beneath it and serves the layer above it) this standard has one more strict rule. Every layer involved in communication from one computer communicates directly with the same layer on the other computer. This means that when you type www.google.com in your browser, there is a direct interaction between your computer's Layer 7 interface (your web browser) and Google.com's web servers (also a Layer 7 interface), and that the same can be said of any other layer.

Keep in mind that there are many opponents today to this model as it doesn't really explain modern Internet design nor the many kinds of network communications. So while it's good for abstract thinking and categorizing, don't expect anything MUST conform to this model. Because many things don't. But it's still a good concept.

So let's first define what are the OSI model layers and their respective responsibilities.

Application Layer	Responsible for direct interaction between applications and the user interface to the application, for instance the use of a web browser like IE or Firefox.
Presentation Layer	Responsible for guaranteeing that data is exchanged in a way that is comprehensible between both parties. In some services that use a form of encryption, the encryption happens at the presentation layer.
Session Layer	Responsible for dialogue control between two computers. Basically it establishes, manages and terminates all connections that happen between the computers.

Transport Layer	Provides transparent transfer of data between computers, providing reliable data transfer services to the upper layers. This means that it is responsible for assembling all data in smaller portions that can be carried reliably on a data network. If a packet is lost or not received, it is the transport layer's job to make sure that that single packet is retransmitted and then reassembled in the correct order.
Network Layer	This layer is responsible for the addressing part of the connection. Not only on ensuring that each address is *unique* on the network, but also on making sure that whatever path is available (whether a good or a bad one), it always delivers the information where it needs to go, and that our information will be sent from hop to hop until it reaches its final destination.
Data Link layer	The data link layer was designed to deal with ensuring the physical layer can recover from errors that might happen and to deal with different connecting mediums. Basically it prepares (encapsulates) data so that it can be transmitted over whatever physical means are necessary (radio waves, fiber-optic cable, copper).
Physical layer	This layer defines the physical specifications of the devices and what needs to be done in order for the information to be transmitted over the selected medium. For a WiFi connection, this is a radio signal; for a fiber connection it's the light being sent; or for a copper connection the electronic signal being sent on the wire.

These seven layers comprise everything that is needed for the reliable communication between computers. However, sometimes security people talk about a **Layer 8** which refers to the users, the people. It's not officially in the model but it does make sense since the users are a huge part of the communication.

Here's how the different models we've discussed look side-by-side:

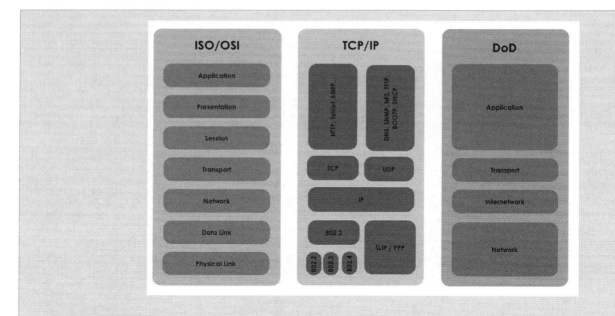

Figure 3.9: Networking Models Compared

Playing with Daemons

Introduction to Daemons

There are thousands of different human languages and dozens of dialects within some of them. You may know several languages yourself, but the odds of you being able to travel across the world and speak to everyone you meet are slim to none.

Yes, you could argue that mathematics is a universal language or music speaks to everyone, but let's be realistic. Try and order a glass of soda with just a little bit of lemon and a scoop of ice cream using those "universal languages" and see how far you get.

If you happen to be in a country where you do not speak the language, please send ISECOM a video of yourself using bagpipes or a saxophone to order a soda. We really want to see that! We may not want to hear it, but we sure do want to see it.

But every day millions of people communicate with one another using a single common language over the Internet. Humans may not all speak the same language; however, our computers and networks do.

The model we use in contemporary networks is the **client-server model.** Physical computers (**hosts** or **servers**) offer **services** (in UNIX they're called **daemons: disk access and execution monitors** – now go impress someone). Think of a web server: it serves up a web page when you ask for it. No mystery.

But actually "you" don't request that page; your web browser does, meaning it's a **client** (or more formally, your computer is). And your computer can be a server, too, at the same time. That's the beauty of networking: you do this for me; I do that for you.

Multiply this model a million times, and you have the Internet. Consider this: millions of computers are offering some kind of service. What does it take to be a client? And is it possible to **subvert** all of this? (Go look up that word if you're not dead certain what it means. This is a hacker course, after all.)

Ready or not, let's dive in.

Services

You have a computer, and you know that there's useful information on it, or you may participate in the common hallucination that you have nothing of digital value. You also know that other people, millions of other people, also have computers and their computers also may have useful information, not to mention handy resources like processors and RAM and disk space and bandwidth.

Now, you can assume that these other people, and these other computers, may very likely have information of interest to someone. The only problem is how to get at all that useful information.

Computers communicate with each other easily through ports, using the protocols we discussed in Lesson 3, but that doesn't really let you read the streams of binary data that computers exchange (unless you have some serious extra time on your hands). You need a way for your computer to get data, interpret it for you, and present it in some form you can use.

The way computers transfer data is through **network services**, or simply **services**. These services allow you to view web pages, exchange email, chat, and interact with remote computers. These services are mapped to port numbers.

Your computer, the **local computer**, uses programs called **clients** to interpret the information that you receive. You might receive information from a **server** (providing a service/running a daemon), over a **TOR** network, from **Torrent seeders** or over **peer-to-peer** networks.

> Of course, your computer can provide services to other remote computers as well, meaning it's a data server or service provider. If you happen to have malware on your computer, you may be providing quite a few services that you don't know about.

Examples of clients include web browsers, email clients, chat programs, Skype, Tor clients, Torrent clients, RSS and so on. These are the applications in the **application layer** of the TCP/IP protocol stack. At the application layer, all the data that is transmitted, encapsulated, encrypted, decrypted, addressed and so forth by the lower layers is turned into something that you, the user, can read and understand.

HTTP and the Web

When we talk about "the Internet," most people are actually thinking of the **World Wide Web**. The World Wide Web, or just the **Web**, isn't the Internet, it's just a small portion of the services available. Usually it just involves viewing web pages through a browser.

> The actual Internet, by the way, consists of all the computers, routers, wires, cable and wireless systems that move all kinds of data around. Only a fraction of this is web traffic.

The web uses **HTTP** or **HyperText Transfer Protocol** and applications (clients) called **web browsers** to access documents on **web servers**. Information from the remote computer is sent to your local computer using the HTTP protocol, usually over port 80. Your web browser interprets that information and renders it on your local computer.

All browsers are not created equal. Each offers different tools and renders HTML content in slightly (or very) different ways. Security and privacy issues may be handled with various degrees of success. This means that you should know what your browser can and can't do, and what settings and plugins give you that perfect balance of security and privacy (unless you like malware, advertisements, spam and your neighborhood knowing that you like to watch kittens play in green jello).

> The **hypertext** part of the HTTP protocol refers to the non-linear way you read it. You normally read in a linear fashion: page 1 then page 2; chapter 1 then chapter 2; lesson 1 then lesson 2, and so on. Hypertext lets you look at information in a non-linear way. You can jump around from topic to topic, learning as you go, then retrace your steps and maybe go see other information before you finish the parent article. That's the difference between hypertext and plain text.

In hypertext, words and ideas connect not only with the words that directly surround them, but also with other words, images, videos, and music. Hypertext isn't restricted to the Web. Most full-featured word processors let you create locally stored pages in web, or HTML, format. You read these pages in your web browser and they act like any other web page, only they are stored on your local computer, not a remote computer.

It's easy to create your own web page. The easiest way to do this is to use one of the common word processors like OpenOffice/LibreOffice Writer, Microsoft Word, or WordPerfect. These programs will allow you to produce simple web pages, combining text, hypertext and images. Plenty of people have made functional web pages using these (or even simple text editors like vi, found on most Unix platforms). Other text editors include Microsoft Notepad, Notepad++, SciTe, emacs and so on.

But these pages aren't flashy. Flashy means **CSS** and **scripts** and animations. You can spend lots of money on fancy web page design applications. These apps allow you to create interesting effects on your web page, but they're more complex to use. Still, they usually make the overall job easier. The lower-cost alternative is to get one of the text editors tailored for working with HTML and scripting languages, learn the syntax of HTML and scripting and code your own web pages from scratch.

Once you have the pages designed, you'll need a computer to put them onto, if you want other people to see them. **Internet Service Providers (ISPs)** provide **web hosting** on their web servers.

You can run a web server from your own home, using your own computer, but there are a whole handful of issues. Information stored on a web server is only available when that server's powered up, operating properly and has an open connection. So if you want to run a web server from your bedroom, you have to leave your computer on all the time; you have to make sure that the web server program is operating properly all the time (this includes troubleshooting hardware problems, controlling viruses, worms and other attacks, and dealing with the inevitable bugs and flaws within the program itself); and you have to keep a connection to the Internet open, which must be stable and fast. ISPs charge extra for a fast upload connection and a fixed IP address, which is why most people pay someone else to do all this.

A web hosting company stores your web pages on their computer. It's nice to let their servers be attacked, instead of yours. A good web hosting company will have multiple, redundant servers and a regular backup policy, so that your site doesn't disappear just because of hardware problems; a support staff keeps servers running despite attacks and program bugs; and a number of open connections to the Internet give some guarantee against outages. So all your have to do is design your web page, upload it to the hosting company's server, turn off your computer and go to sleep. Your web page will be available to the entire world, as long as you keep paying the bill.

It's also possible to find organizations that offer free web hosting. Some of these organizations are funded by paid advertising, which means that anyone who wants to view your web page will first have to view someone else's advertisement. But they won't have to buy anything, and you won't have to pay anything.

Exercises

4.1 A web page is just text that tells the browser where images, videos, and other things should be. You can see what it looks like by viewing the Page Source. Go to your favorite browser, point it at ISECOM.ORG and load the page. Now view the source. You'll see some tags with the word "meta" in them. For example, the first is meta-charset="utf-8". What does that mean? What is the point of it?

4.2 Find 3 more meta tags and explain what the point of them is. You may need to search around the web to figure it out so think carefully about what key words you will use in your search to make sure you get the right answers.

4.3 Save the ISECOM.ORG Page Source to your computer. Drag it to the browser. What changed? Why do you think it changed?

4.4 Open the ISECOM.ORG Page Source in a text editor and you'll see it's just words and numbers. Whatever you change or type in there will affect how the page looks when you save it and drag it back into the web browser. Delete things and you'll see it deleted. Change words and they will appear as you typed them. Now strip the page of anything else and add your name so it shows up larger and bolder than the other words. Try it. Save it. And drag it to the web browser and see if you were successful. No? Then keep trying!

*See the **Feed Your Head: Playing With HTTP** at the end of this lesson for an opportunity to dig deeper.*

Email – SMTP, POP and IMAP

The second most visible aspect of the Internet is probably email. On your computer you use an email client, which connects to a mail server. When you set up your email account, you get a unique name in the form of **user@domain** and you have to create a password.

There are two parts to email: **SMTP (Simple Mail Transfer Protocol)**, which *sends* mail, and the mail server, either **POP (Post Office Protocol)** or **IMAP (Internet Message Access Protocol)**, which *retrieves* your email.

The SMTP protocol (we'll remind you again) is used to *send* email. SMTP defines the **fields** in an email message, including the FROM, TO, SUBJECT, CC and BODY fields. Plain old SMTP does not require a password and sends everything in clear text; everybody gets to read your mail. This may not have been bad when the protocol was designed and the Internet was a small world inhabited by like-minded people. But it left a loophole that allowed any user to send **spam** and do other nasty things like **email spoofing**, which basically means lying about (spoofing) the sending address. Almost all contemporary mail servers use Secure SMTP, which means you must prove your identity before you can send an email.

In later lessons we'll show you how spoofing works and how to look for it in email headers. This bit of knowledge can turn you from the sheep to the wolf awfully quickly.

POP3 (Post Office Protocol version 3) is a "store and dump" protocol. The email server receives your email and stores it for you, until you connect and download (dump) your email. Then your outgoing mail is sent using SMTP. This is a good way to approach email if you have a dial-up connection, since it takes less time to send and receive email, and you can read your email offline.

IMAP, on the other hand, by default stores your mail on the server. Many corporate email solutions use a form of IMAP, depending on their software vendors. In IMAP, you can create folders in your mailbox and move messages between these folders. When you connect to the IMAP server, your mailboxes and the server synchronize the folders, contents, incoming email and deleted email. This has quite an advantage: you can get to all your mail from any computer or device you use: laptop, kiosk, phone or tablet. Plus you can download and store email in personal data files on your own computer.

However, there are also two drawbacks: first, obviously, is that you need to exchange more information, so you need a faster connection and more time. The second is that space is limited. Your mail server will assign you a mailbox size that you can't exceed. If you run out of space, you won't be able to receive messages unless you delete emails (or pay for more space). Ultimately this means that corporate IMAP email requires data management. You have to move mail to local storage and clean out your sent mail, spam, and trash on a regular basis to conserve space. Mail with attachments will destroy you. In this age of free Internet email accounts with huge free data storage, all this upkeep may seem stupid. Until you get sued. Or someone compromises the mail server and gets ALL your email.

Both POP and IMAP servers require a password to access your account. But both protocols send *everything* in the clear, including passwords, so anyone can potentially read them. You have to use some form of encryption to mask the login process (like SSL) and the contents of the mail. That's why many email clients have a *Use SSL* check box.

When you click the Send button in your email client, two things happen: first your client forces you to log in to the SMTP server (even though you've already logged in to the POP server, dang it!), and then it sends your outgoing mail (via the SMTP protocol).

This got annoying by the mid-1990s, when servers began to use a protocol called **POP-before-SMTP**: you first send the POP server your user name and password, then your incoming mail downloads, then the SMTP server checks you against the POP server ("Is this guy okay?" "Yeah, I authenticated him.") and sends your messages. It's a nice time-saver.

One important item to remember is, despite being password protected, email is not a way to send secure information. Most POP clients and servers require that your password be communicated – unencrypted – to your mail server. This doesn't mean than anyone who receives an email from you also receives your password; but it does mean that someone with the right knowledge and tools can sniff out your password – as well as the contents of your emails. (For ideas on making your email more secure, see **Lesson 9: Email Security**.)

Exercises

4.5   Send yourself an email from your main account, to your main account. Send the same email to your same main account from another account, for instance a free online account (come on, we know you have them). How long do the two messages take to arrive? If there is a difference, why?

4.6   Look at one of the billions of spam emails that clog your inbox. Can you determine who actually sent you a particular email? Is there any kind of hidden information in emails, for instance? If there is, how can a clever hacker see it?

4.7   Can you delay the sending of an email until a certain time or day (which can really screw up Deniability)? Can you think of cool way to use email sending delays to mess with your friends?

IRC

IRC (Internet Relay Chat) is a great place to see the unregulated nature of the Internet at its best. Or worst. On IRC, anyone with anything to say gets a chance to say it. IRC is also known as **Usenet** or **news groups**. Each news group has its own name, sub-name, sub-sub-name and so forth.

You may be familiar with chat rooms. IRC is just like a chat room, only there are no rules beyond basic **netiquette**, and quite often there are no chaperones. You may find exactly what you are looking for on an IRC channel, or you may find something you never knew existed.

All the rules that you've heard about chat rooms are applicable to IRC channels. Don't tell anyone your real name. Don't give out your phone number, your address, or your bank account numbers. But have fun! If you are roaming around, be careful about the content available. Not everything on the Internet is malware-free, and not everyone on the Internet is nice.

IRC is not secure and everything you type is passed in clear text from IRC server to IRC server. You can set up private conversations between yourself and another IRC member but those are transmitted in the clear as well. Using a nickname will only get you a little privacy. If you're planning on conducting any malicious or unsavory actions, don't use the same nickname for every account. Using the same nickname is an excellent way of getting tracked down by the police. Or much less savory people.

Topics are called "channels." Since there are thousands of channels, we'll give you a URL that lists many of them for you to pursue until you lose your mind:

```
http://www.nic.funet.fi/~irc/channels.html
```

If you are having problems with the comments made by another member, you can either report them to the moderator (if there is one), or have that person **bumped** from that channel. If you don't want to hear what someone has to say, you can always block them or ignore their messages. Maybe that thread's not for you anyway.

Exercises

4.8   Find three IRC channels that focus on security topics. How do you join in the public conversation? What do you have to do to have a private conversation with a person?

4.9   What port does IRC use?

4.10   It is possible to exchange files through IRC. How do you do this? Would you *want* to exchange files through IRC?

4.11   What's the major difference between MIME and SMIME? When you see an "S" in an acronym, does that mean anything special to you as a *Secure* (hint, hint) minded person?

FTP

Old-school **File Transfer Protocol (FTP)** typically runs over ports 20 and 21. Guess what: it lets you transfer files between two computers. While it can be used for private file transfers, because it doesn't use encryption it's more commonly used for free, anonymous FTP servers that offer public access to collections of files, like the ISO for that cool new Linux distro.

Anonymous FTP was once the main way for computer users to exchange files over the Internet. While there are plenty of anonymous FTP servers used to distribute files illegally (which is a nice way to spread binary disease), more are legally used to distribute programs and files. You can find servers that offer anonymous FTP services through the usual methods, for instance search engines. But remember: FTP logins are sent in clear-text. Yes, even though we're talking about a user name and password. (Is that lame or what?) There is secure FTP (SFTP) but it's not universally used.

Most anonymous FTP servers allow you to access their files using the FTP protocol through a web browser. There are also some really great FTP clients that work like a file management program. Once you're logged into the FTP server, you can move files onto your computer in much the same way you move files on your own computer. FTP just takes a bit longer to download each file over your computer, mainly because the FTP server may be located on the other side of the planet.

Exercises

4.12   Windows, OSX and Linux come with a basic command line FTP client; to access it, open a command prompt or terminal window and type:

```
ftp
```

At the `ftp>` prompt, you can type `help`, to get a list of available commands.

```
ftp> help
```

```
Commands may be abbreviated.  Commands are:
!              delete         literal        prompt         send
?              debug          ls             put            status
append         dir            mdelete        pwd            trace
ascii          disconnect     mdir           quit           type
bell           get            mget           quote          user
binary         glob           mkdir          recv           verbose
bye            hash           mls            remotehelp
cd             help           mput           rename
close          lcd            open           rmdir
```

The basic commands are:

Connect to the FTP server named *ftp.domain.name*:

```
ftp> open ftp.domain.name
```

List the contents of the remote working directory:

```
ftp> ls
```

   or

```
ftp> dir
```

Change the remote working directory to a directory named *newdir*:

```
ftp> cd newdir
```

Download a file named *filename* from the remote computer to the local computer:

```
ftp> get filename
```

Download multiple files named *file1*, *file2*, and *file3* from the remote computer to the local computer (you can also use wildcards to download many files with the same suffix, or all the files in a directory):

```
ftp> mget file1 file2 file3
```

Uploads a file named *filename* from the local computer to the remote computer:

```
ftp> put filename
```

Disconnect from the remote FTP server:

```
ftp> close
```

Shut down your local FTP client:

```
ftp> quit
```

An FTP session, step by step

To connect to an anonymous ftp service, first open your local FTP client:

```
ftp
```

Use the open command to connect to the server. The command

```
ftp> open anon.server
```

connects your FTP client with the anonymous FTP server named *anon.server*. Substitute the name of a real server, of course.

When the remote FTP server accepts your connection, it will identify itself to your local client, then ask for a user name.

```
Connected to anon.server.
220 ProFTPD Server (Welcome . . . )
User (anon.server:(none)):
```

For most anonymous FTP servers, you should enter in the word *anonymous* (or *ftp*) as the user name. The remote FTP server will acknowledge that you are connecting as an anonymous user, and will give you instructions on what to use as a password.

```
331 Anonymous login ok, send your complete email address as your
password.
Password:
```

In most cases, the remote server does not check the validity of the email address entered as a password, so it will not stop you from accessing the service if you enter an invalid address. This is considered to be a breach of netiquette, but it's actually necessary: do not give away your real email address! After you have entered a password, the remote server will send a welcome message to your local computer.

```
230-
        Welcome   to   ftp.anon.server,   the   public   ftp   server   of
anon.server. We
   hope you find what you're looking for.
   If you have any problems or questions, please send email to
   ftpadmin@anon.server
   Thanks!
230 Anonymous access granted, restrictions apply.
```

From here, you can use the ls, dir, cd and get commands to download files from the remote server to your local computer.

Exercises

4.13   Using these examples, find and download a file from an anonymous FTP server.

4.14   Use your web browser and a search engine to find an anonymous FTP server that has a copy of *Alice in Wonderland*, then, using the command line FTP client – not your web browser – download the file.

4.15   What are the better FTP clients out there? Can they automate all the command-line stuff and provide you a nice graphical interface? Do you lose any functionality you have at the command line?

4.16   Could your computer become an FTP server?

Telnet and SSH

Telnet allows a local user to send a wide variety of commands to a remote computer. This allows the local user to instruct the remote computer to perform functions and return data to the local computer, almost as if you were sitting at a keyboard in front of the remote computer. **Secure Shell (SSH)** is intended as a secure, encrypted replacement for clear-text telnet.

Again, most Windows, OSX and Linux versions come with a basic, command line telnet client; to access it, open a command prompt or terminal window and type:

```
telnet
```

To access a telnet server, you will need to have an account and password set up for you by the administrator of the server, because the telnet program lets you do lot of things, some of which could severely compromise the remote computer.

Telnet was used back in the day to allow computer administrators to remotely control servers and to provide user support from a distance. This service is part of the old Internet and isn't used much anymore.

Telnet can also be used for a number of other tasks, such as sending and receiving email and viewing the source code for web pages (although telnet is probably the most difficult way to do these things). Many of these things are legitimate, but they can be abused for illegal or immoral reasons. You can use telnet to check your email, and view, not just the subject line, but the first few lines of an email, which will allow you to decide whether or not to delete the email without downloading the entire message.

If you are going to use SSH, be sure you're using a current version, because older versions had various vulnerabilities, and many automatic vulnerability scanners constantly search for these on the Internet.

 Game On: Command Me

The dark screen twinkled across the front of Grandpa's thick glasses as the cursor blinked impatiently, expecting a command. With his gray thin hair lapped lazily over his wrinkled head, Grandpa tapped the keyboard. Jace watched the silent piano player play the keys of his computer, tap, tap, tap, tap. He smiled at Jace with his head turned to look into her young eyes. "Jace, I'm going to show you a new world out there. Buckle your seatbelt," he winked at the eight year old.

Jace's feet barely reached the floor in the computer chair with her grandfather behind the computer screen. She heard the telephone dial tone coming from a small box close by. The white box lit up with green and red lights as the tone changed to a sound like a duck being swallowed by a garbage disposal. Grandpa raised his excited eyebrows and stared with all of his might at the black screen in front of him. The duck stopped wailing and all of the lights turned green on the telephone box.

Grandpa said, "Watch this."

Usually when Grandpa said, "watch this" something would explode or black smoke would come from something. Either way, "watch this" meant Grandma was going to mad about something he did wrong. Jace loved to hear those words though, because it was exciting anticipation for some wonderful event.

The computer screen woke up from its dark slumber with a banner of ASCII text surrounding the words "Welcome to Cline's Bulletin Board System (BBS)." "We're in," Grandpa clapped and attempted to high-five eight year old Jace. His hands missed her hand by several inches and he almost smacked the little girl in her face. She laughed, and Grandpa did too.

They both looked back and forth at the keyboard and the computer screen. Grandpa rubbed his fingers together while Jace rubbed her mind, trying to figure out what was going on. Grandpa began typing commands on the silent piano, head bowed down over the keys as a vulture might eat roadkill. Head up, head down, head up, head. Oops. He sat back. Grandpa had forgotten something very important.

He paused and spoke like a teacher. "Jace, I'm sorry but I forgot to tell you what's going on here. Right now, I am connected to another computer over our telephone line. That noisy thing over there is called a "Modem" and its job is to convert digital signals to analog and vice versa." Jace already knew way too much about telephone systems due to Grandpa's desire to play around with it every chance he could. 48 volts during normal use and 90 volts during a telephone ring notification, she knew more than any telephone technician needed to know. Plain old telephone system or POTS was a joke between Grandpa and herself. Grandma didn't seem to get the POTS joke which made it that much funnier.

Telephone lines can be tapped by an interested party, but that could be detected by using a voltage regulator. The telephone line voltage would spike momentarily and keep slightly elevated if someone tried to tap the line. Jace thought that Grandpa loved his voltmeter more than he loved Grandma; he never left home without it. Grandpa even went so far as to name his device "Valerie." Valerie the voltmeter. That was his best friend, besides Jace.

Jace rolled her smarty-pants eyes at the Grandpa, more so at the lecture on analog modulation to digital modulation, converting sound to a digital signal. That's pretty much what a modem does. Grandpa continued his lecture to the reluctant student, "The computer I'm connected to allows me to connect to other computers and play around with whatever services they provide." Her ears picked up a word that she hadn't heard before, "services."

"Grandpa what do you mean 'services?'" the curious girl asked expecting an answer involving fast food. "Excellent question, my dear," Grandpa was expecting Jace to ask a question like that. "My computer is connected to a network of computers or I have the ability to connect to other computers across the world," he gladly replied. "This modem lets me talk to these other computers that offer access to files, information, people to talk with, and wonderful stuff like that. These computers offer services like File Transport Protocol, Usenet, IRC, Telnet, and Email."

Jace wasn't satisfied with the answer she was given and this usually led to many more questions fired at Grandpa in rapid succession. She loaded up her question ammo belt and began the carnage: "What is File Tranfer proto thing? What is MIC? Where is Telknit? Does Imail need special stamps? What color is it in the digital world? Who invented Usednet? Why do they call it Imail? Does Grandma know about your services? Why do they call it services? Where do babies come from? Where does Jello come from?"

Grandpa had to cover his ears to shelter his brain from the onslaught of questions. "Wait, wait, wait, slow down."

Game Over

DNS

When you want to call a friend on the phone, you need to know the correct phone number; when you want to connect to a remote computer, you also need to know its number. You may remember from previous lessons that, for computers on the Internet, this number is the IP address.

IP addresses are very easily managed by computers, but we humans prefer to use names, in this case **domain names**. For example, to connect to the Hacker Highschool website, type www.hackerhighschool.org into the address bar of a web browser. However, the web browser can't use this name to connect to the server that hosts the Hacker Highschool website – it needs the IP address. This means that your local computer must have some means of translating domain names into IP addresses. If there were only hundreds, or even thousands of computers on the Internet, then it might be possible for you to have a simple table (a **hosts file**) stored on your computer to use to look up these addresses. However, for better or worse, not only are there millions of computers on the Internet, but the correlations between domain names and IP addresses change constantly.

Domain Name Service (DNS) is used to dynamically translate domain names into IP addresses (and vice-versa). When you type the domain name *www.domainname.com* into your web browser, your web browser contacts the DNS server chosen by your ISP. If that DNS server has *www.domainname.com* in its database, then it returns the IP address to your computer, allowing you to connect.

If your DNS server doesn't have *www.domainname.com* in its database, then it sends a request to another DNS server, and they will keep sending requests to other DNS servers until one finds the correct IP address, or establishes that the domain name is invalid.

Exercises

4.17   Open a command line window and identify the IP address of your computer. What command have you used? What IP address do you have?

4.18   Identify the IP address of your DNS server. What command have you used? What is the IP address of the DNS server?

4.19   Ping *www.isecom.org*. Do you receive an answer? What IP address answers the ping?

4.20   Can you direct your computer to use a different DNS server? If so, change the configuration of your computer so that it uses a different DNS server. Search for free DNS servers online. Ping *www.isecom.org* again. Do you receive the same response? Why?

4.21   On a Windows computer, open the CLI and try the IPCONFIG command. It does many things but for DNS, it lets you see the cache where you've been and you can also erase it. Show here what you typed to do those things.

4.22   On a Linux computer at the CLI, you can use the command DIG to investigate DNS servers. Another tool is WHOIS. What are each of the tools used for? Show what you typed for those comands to investigate DNS.

DHCP

DHCP or **Dynamic Host Configuration Protocol** allows a local network server to hand out IP addresses within the network. The server is given a block of IP addresses to use. When a computer joins the network, it gets an IP address. When a computer leaves, its IP address becomes available for use by another computer.

This is useful for large networks of computers, since it's not necessary for each computer to have an individually assigned, static IP address. Instead, you use a DHCP server. When a new computer connects to the network, the first thing that it does is request an IP address from the DHCP server. Once it has been assigned an IP address, the computer then has access to all the services of the network.

Now think about that. Most wifi networks offer DHCP, meaning that *anyone* can get an IP address on that subnet. If you're running a coffee shop that's exactly what you want, but if you're running a secure office, you might consider using fixed IP addresses instead. It depends....

 Game On: You've Got My Number

Jace remembered those talks with Grandpa, his humor, and his voltmeter named Valerie. She smiled and her heart warmed up even though she was mad as hell. She pounded her fists on the computer table in anger and frustration. A voice from the front of the room stupidly asked, "Is there a problem, Ms. Jace?"

Of course there's a problem you pinhead, she thought. "Yes, Mr. Tri, I'm having a difficult time keeping a connection open on this machine. I keep being bounced off the Internet," the bitter teen squeezed the words between her clenched teeth.

Her brain kicked her in the head, "Why did you say anything? He's just going to mess it up even more." The high school student held her hand up to stop Mr. Tri's approach towards her. She wanted to yell "STOP" at him but the calamity was in motion, like a train wreck in slow motion. Mr. Tri pushed desks, chairs and students out of his way to intercept the young hacker as quickly as he could. Jace closed her eyes, bracing for the impact of what was going to happen.

"Well, Ms. Jace, what seems to be the problem now? Have you been snooping into student report cards, erasing your bad grades, or purchasing items off of Tree Bay using a stolen credit card?" he accused her. Dried snot crusted the outside of his nose as he peered over her head at the monitor. She could hear and smell his wheezing breath with the stench of old fish innards that made her own nose protest. Her gag reflexes forced a small amount of vomit into her mouth so she moved her face away from the decay towards the fresh air of the ceiling fan above.

Jace breathed out of her mouth and said, "Mr. Tri, it's no big deal. I'm just being bumped off of my connection, every few minutes." When someone talks without taking in air from their nose, they sound like they have a cold or sinus problems. Mr. Stench replied, "Well, check the power cord. Maybe it's loose. You can also look at the cable between the computer and the monitor." Crash!! The train wreck continued in slow motion. Like finger nails on a chalkboard, Jace winced at his horrible advice.

To slow down the pending casualties of the train crash, Jace tried her hardest to deflect his stupidity. "Sir, the computer connections are fine. I think someone is sharing the same IP address as I am. We are bumping each other off every time one of us attempts to connect to a network service," she almost pleaded as a convicted killer might plead to a judge. "Two networked devices can't share the same IP address when they are both trying to use network services like FTP, Telnet, Usenet, HTTP, or IRC. Each device must have its own IP address, which acts like a location beacon, to the local server or router. When a computer sends out a request for a service, the routing needs to know which computer made that request and where to send the service reply to."

The crash was beginning to slow down; the crash might even be a small one for a train wreck. Mr. Tri snorted as some tuna fish launched out of his mouth and landed on Jace's shoulder. "If I am sharing the same IP address with someone else, the network doesn't know where to send the data to," Jace reasoned to the stumped teacher.

"Well Ms. Jace, I certainly know where to send you. How about detention after another visit with your best friend the Vice Principal," he blurted at the too intelligent teen.

Game Over

Connections

In the bad old days, computers connected to the Internet through a modem. Modems translate bits into sounds and back, **mod**ulating and **dem**odulating, thus the name. Modem speeds are measured in **baud** (a rating number) and **bps**, or bits per second. Higher baud rates usually mean higher bps, but you must also consider what you are planning to do. There are certain applications – such as telnetting into **Multi-User Dungeons (MUDs)** – for which a twenty year old 300 baud modem would still be acceptable (provided your typing speed wasn't so good), while high bandwidth applications such as streaming video can often strain even the most powerful cable or DSL connections.

ISPs

You don't just call up the Internet. You need to access a server that will connect your computer to the Internet. The server does all the heavy work, and is on all the time. The server is run by an **Internet Service Provider (ISP)**.

An ISP has a point-of-presence on the Internet that is constant, and it has servers that run services you can use. But you can run these services on your own, too. For example, you can run a mail server on your local computer, but it will require you to have your computer powered up and connected to a network all the time, just waiting for those brief moments when information has to be exchanged. An ISP, however, consolidates the efforts of a large number of users, so the mail server is working all the time, instead of sitting around, doing nothing. The ISP's computers use a high speed connection to connect to a **Network Access Point (NAP)**. These NAPs then interconnect with each other through ultra-high speed connections called **backbones**. All these things together are the Internet.

Plain Old Telephone Service

Plain old telephone service (POTS) was once the most widely used method of accessing the Internet. Its primary disadvantage is its low speed, but in many cases this is made up for by its wide availability. Most national Internet service providers have a large number of local access numbers, and almost everyone still has a phone with a land line. In theory, if you had an acoustic modem and a pocket full of change, you could connect from almost any public pay phone (if you can find one). Not that you would really want to do that.

POTS is slow. The fastest telephone modems are rated at a speed of 56,600 bits per second (bps). That, however, as they explain in the small print, is a lie. Power constraints limit the actual download speed to about 53,000 bps and the effective rate is usually much lower. This doesn't compare very well with DSL or cable modems.

That said, telephone service is widely available, and POTS based ISPs are relatively cheap (and sometimes free). You wouldn't want to trade pirated movies over POTS, because it's immoral, illegal and ties up your phone line all night and maybe all weekend, but you could certainly send friendly, text based emails to Granny. And if you used telnet, you could even do it with a dusty DOS based machine that you pulled out of the basement.

DSL

A **Digital Subscriber Line (DSL)** is a method of sending large amounts of information over the wires that already exist for POTS. Its main advantage over POTS is that it is much faster than analog modems, and it provides a permanent connection. In addition, it allows you to make and receive regular telephone calls while you are connected to the Internet. Its main disadvantage is that its availability is limited by how close you are to the telephone company's switching equipment – if you live too far down the line, you're out of luck.

Cable Modems

Cable gateways don't use traditional telephone lines to connect to the Internet. Instead they use coaxial cable (or fiber-optic lines, if you're really lucky) provided by cable companies. Like DSL, cable gateways can allow you to make and receive regular telephone calls while you are connected to the Internet, and they provide a permanent connection, but cable gateways are generally faster than DSL.

Cable gateways have some basic flaws. The first is that cable gateway access is a shared resource, so your connection speed will be decreased when there are other users on the same cable with you. The second is that cable access is only available in areas where cable companies have installed the necessary wiring. And the most serious one is that any traffic you put on the cable can be viewed by any other user on that cable! This means that if you connect your computer to the cable gateway and do not use a firewall, everyone else in the neighborhood can see your computer and all its files. Do you really want to share your bank account information like that?

Wimax

Wimax is a wireless connection method that generally competes with DSL. It is used in places where a wired infrastructure would be too expensive or difficult to setup. Signal strength can be affected by buildings, trees or other large objects. Some versions use a fixed access point, but others give you mobile access over truly large areas.

Wifi

Wifi is not a method to connect to your ISP but it is a common networking method for connecting to the Internet at home or at commercial establishments like malls or coffee shops. Most smartphones and all laptops now use Wifi so it's a favorite target for attackers. Consider yourself naked in a crowded room when you use public Wifi: cover yourself, make sure nobody's looking at you but assume everybody wants to. Of course you will read the Wireless Security lesson too, right?

 Game On: At Your Service

The bedroom air circulated a smell somewhere between flower perfume and dirty socks. The decor of Jace's bedroom matched the smell. Neither Mokoa nor Jace were concerned over the computing environment, both just wanted the get their task done.

After three minutes of constant chatter, babbling to Mokoa, the teen had enough. Mokoa gazed at the computer monitor as if he had bloodshot eyes and was forced to view boredom in two dimensions. He slapped his own forehead in frustration.

"And what does any of this have to do with me?" Mokoa pleaded. He slumped his head downward, surrendering any hope to learn from his computer teacher, Jace. "This is soooo boring. Who cares about this old computer lingo and ancient machine code," he begged.

Jace stopped talking.

As a lion might eye its dinner before the quick kill, she slowly turned her tight-jawed head towards her impatient student. Jace considered throwing her monitor on top of Mokoa's head, or slapping him across his face with her keyboard. Jace had plenty of options.

Instead of physical violence, she simply acted as if she were speaking to a young

Mokoa.

"The reason I am telling you about FTP, Telnet, IRC VOIP, and all these other services is because you are a knucklehead. You need to know about these networking functions since they are still in use today. Before we had 'Text Me, Please' and 'Post Your Life Online,' which all make money by marketing your personal information, we used other services. These older services are free, and they are still available."

Jace looked around her small desk and grabbed a wooden ruler. Mokoa sprung up and backed away from Jace, expecting to be whacked with the ruler.

"When you think of the Internet, think of it as this ruler. This ruler is just so long but it is broken up into smaller segments."

Mokoa nodded using his arms to protect his face from the imminent wooden ruler attack.

Jace growled at Mokoa as he squirmed to keep his distance from her. "Most people think the Internet is the World Wide Web. It's not; in fact WWW is a very small part of the Internet. If you think of this ruler as the Internet, WWW is only one half a segment of the whole ruler. The rest of the ruler is made up of tons of other services, databases, catalogs, and stuff like that."

Mokoa uncovered his face enough to see Jace sitting while holding the ruler between her two thumbs and index fingers. She was not holding the object as a weapon; she was using it as a teaching tool.

Feeling a bit more relaxed, Mokoa sat back down next to Jace as she returned to teaching mode.

"A vast majority of the Internet is hidden from users because it is made up of private or academic databases. What we can access, are all the original portions that make the Internet so useful," Jace said just as she swatted Mokoa across his thighs with the ruler.

Game Over

Exercises

4.23   What kind of Internet connection do you have at home, if you have one? How can you tell? And most important:

4.24   Who can you see on that network? (How can you find out?)

4.25   How fast is your connection? Can you improve your speed without calling up your ISP?

4.26   What additional services does your ISP provide? We talked about services already; your ISP may support several.

4.27   What services can you provide from your own computer?

Feed Your Head: Playing With HTTP

HTTP, the acronym for Hypertext Transfer Protocol, is located on the top of TCP/IP stack as is defined in two main RFC:

- 1945 for 1.0 (based from 0.9).

- 2616 for 1.1.

There are some substantial upgrades and differences from 1.0 to 1.1 for Extensibility, Caching, Bandwidth optimization, Network connection management, Message transmission, Internet address conservation, Error notification, Security, integrity, and authentication, Content negotiation [3]. Differences between 1.0 and 1.1 are useful to obtain information about a web server.

Basically HTTP is a stateless protocol in which Client sends an HTTP Request to Server, which sends an HTTP Response: the Request/Response paradigm.

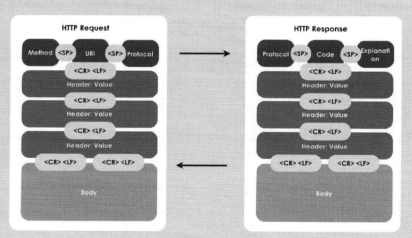

Figure 4.1: *HTTP*

As you may know we can obtain a lot of information sending commands to an HTTP server. We will use some basic network tools:

- netcat: the TCP/IP tool kit

- curl: the HTTP tool kit

- proxy: like OWASP ZAP or Burpsuite free

Sniffing the Connection Between You and the HHS HTTP Server

Use a proxy to connect your browser. Go to http://www.hackerhighschool.org and intercept your request:

```
GET / HTTP/1.1
Host: www.hackerhighschool.org
User-Agent:  Mozilla/5.0  (Macintosh;  Intel  Mac  OS  X  10.8;
rv:11.0) Gecko/20100101 Firefox/11.0
Accept:
text/html,application/xhtml+xml,application/xml;q=0.9,*/*;q=0.8
Accept-Language: en-us,en;q=0.5
Accept-Encoding: gzip, deflate
Proxy-Connection: keep-alive
```

and response:

```
HTTP/1.1 200 OK
Content-Length: 10376
Date: Fri, 03 Feb 2013 09:11:17 GMT
Server: Apache/2.2.22
Last-Modified: Mon, 06 Feb 2013 09:31:18 GMT
ETag: "2f42-4b8485316c580"
Accept-Ranges: bytes
Identity: The Institute for Security and Open Methodologies, The
Institute for Security and Open Methodologies
P3P: Not supported at this time, Not supported at this time
Content-Type: text/html
Connection: keep-alive

<!DOCTYPE html PUBLIC "-//W3C//DTD XHTML 1.0 Transitional//EN"
"http://www.w3.org/TR/xhtml1/DTD/xhtml1-
transitional.dtd"[]><html    xmlns="http://www.w3.org/1999/xhtml"
dir="ltr"     lang="en-US"     xml:lang="en"><head><meta     http-
equiv="Content-Type"      content="text/html;      charset=UTF-8"
/><title>Hacker    Highschool   -   Security   Awareness   for
Teens</title>
[...]
```

Exercises

4.28   Identify parts of requests from proxy using the diagrams.

4.29   Is there interesting information in the headers?

Your First Manual Connection

Netcat can be used to connect to a web server using host port settings.

Start by typing:

```
nc www.hackerhighschool.org 80
```

Then press Enter two times.

```
GET / HTTP/1.0
```

The server will reply:

```
<!DOCTYPE html PUBLIC "-//W3C//DTD XHTML 1.0 Transitional//EN"
"http://www.w3.org/TR/xhtml1/DTD/xhtml1-transitional.dtd"[]>
<html  xmlns="http://www.w3.org/1999/xhtml"  dir="ltr"  lang="en-
US" xml:lang="en"><head>
<meta http-equiv="Content-Type" content="text/html; charset=UTF-
8" />
<title>ISECOM     -     Institute     for     Security     and     Open
Methodologies</title>            <meta          name="description"
content="Description" />
```

As you can see the page appears to be from isecom.org and not from hackerhighschool.org. Why?

One hypothesis could be that the same host serves up both HHS the ISECOM site. Is this possible?

To find out, check the hackerhighschool.org IP address:

```
nslookup www.hackerhighschool.org
[...]
Non-authoritative answer:
www.hackerhighschool.org canonical name = hackerhighschool.org.
Name:      hackerhighschool.org
Address: 216.92.116.13
```

And now for www.isecom.org:

```
nslookup isecom.org
[...]
```

```
Non-authoritative answer:
Name:      isecom.org
Address: 216.92.116.13
```

Same IP address! Using netcat it's possible to show the host by manually adding the Host header and using HTTP 1.1:

```
GET / HTTP/1.1
Host: www.hackerhighschool.org

HTTP/1.1 200 OK
Content-Length: 10376
Date: Fri, 03 Feb 2013 09:11:17 GMT
Server: Apache/2.2.22
Last-Modified: Mon, 06 Feb 2013 09:31:18 GMT
ETag: "2f42-4b8485316c580"
Accept-Ranges: bytes
Identity: The Institute for Security and Open Methodologies, The
Institute for Security and Open Methodologies
P3P: Not supported at this time, Not supported at this time
Content-Type: text/html
Connection: keep-alive
<!DOCTYPE html PUBLIC "-//W3C//DTD XHTML 1.0 Transitional//EN"
"http://www.w3.org/TR/xhtml1/DTD/xhtml1-transitional.dtd"[]>
<html xmlns="http://www.w3.org/1999/xhtml" dir="ltr" lang="en-
US" xml:lang="en"><head>
<meta http-equiv="Content-Type" content="text/html; charset=UTF-
8" />
<title>Hacker Highschool - Security Awareness for Teens</title>
```

The Request Method

Another part of an HTTP request that can be modified is the Request Method. Typically web applications use GET and POST requests, but other request protocols may be active on a web server or application server. Common methods are:

- **OPTIONS** - used to ask what request options are supported.
  If you're running a web server, be aware that giving this information away could be a problem.

- **GET** - used to retrieve information directly via the URL, for example:
  `http://www.usairnet.com/cgi-bin/launch/code.cgi?`
  `Submit=Go&sta=KSAF&state=NM`

See all that stuff after the question mark? That's the request data. Passing data this way is risky, because it's in plain sight, and it's easy to tinker with.

- **HEAD** - used like GET but the server does not return an actual page.
  This can be used to identify Accesses, optimizing bandwidth consumption and – in some cases – bypassing access controls. In fact some ACL implementations check only GET requests. In this case you have found a Vulnerability.

- **POST** - used to send data to web applications – like GET – but data is transmitted in the Request Body, out of sight to at least a degree.

- **PUT** - used to allocate resources on a web server or to update it.
  In many contexts this method should have been disabled or protected by an Authentication Control. In other contexts this is a delightful find.

- **DELETE** - used to free resources on a web server.
  This method should be disabled or protected by an Authentication Control. See PUT above.

- **TRACE** - used as an application layer loopback that reflects messages.
  This debug method should be disabled, in particular on production environment because is a Confidentiality Concern and introduces a Vulnerability because it can be used for Cross Site Scripting exploits.

- **CONNECT** – to use the web server as a proxy.
  This should be disabled or protected by an Authentication Control because it permits others to connect to third party services using the proxy IP.

Also consider more protocols based on HTTP can adds more methods, as WebDAV. You can alter Request Method in order to look at server replies for interesting stuff, asking for known methods and also arbitrary words.

Requesting OPTIONS

You could start the netcat session as usual:

```
# nc www.hackerhighschool.org 80
```

But don't press Enter twice this time. Instead, type the next line:

```
OPTIONS / HTTP/1.1
```

and you'll get a response like:

```
Host: www.hackerhighschool.org
HTTP/1.0 200 OK
Date: Tue, 07 Feb 2013 08:43:38 GMT
Server: Apache/2.2.22
Allow: GET,HEAD,POST,OPTIONS
Identity: The Institute for Security and Open Methodologies, The
Institute for Security and Open Methodologies
P3P: Not supported at this time, Not supported at this time
Content-Length: 0
Content-Type: text/html
```

Requesting HEAD

This time, after starting your session, enter the HEAD option.

```
# nc www.hackerhighschool.org 80
HEAD / HTTP/1.1
Host: www.hackerhighschool.org

HTTP/1.0 200 OK
Date: Tue, 07 Feb 2013 08:41:14 GMT
Server: Apache/2.2.22
Last-Modified: Fri, 13 Feb 2013 15:48:14 GMT
ETag: "3e3a-4bd916679ab80"
Accept-Ranges: bytes
Content-Length: 15930
Identity: The Institute for Security and Open Methodologies
P3P: Not supported at this time
Content-Type: text/html
Age: 45
Connection: close
```

Let Me Use You As A Proxy: the CONNECT Request

```
# nc www.hackerhighschool.org 80
CONNECT http://www.isecom.org/ HTTP/1.1
Host: www.hackerhighschool.org
```

Exercise

4.30   Use netcat (nc) to try all of the Request methods listed above on the HHS network servers or a server set up for the purpose. What kind of interesting stuff can you dig up?

Scripting HTTP requests with curl

Some Web Application Testing is based not only to Web Server response but on the (Web) Application Layer. Often you can find web application vulnerabilities by altering GET and POST parameters, altering cookies and tinkering with headers. A useful tool, for bash scripting is the **curl** command, a command-line tool for requesting a web page. But curl adds some logic over netcat.

Asking for:

```
# curl http://www.isecom.org
```

is not the same as

```
# nc www.isecom.org 80
GET / HTTP/1.1
```

To see this you can use the -v switch for verbose output:

```
# curl -v http://www.isecom.org/
* About to connect() to www.isecom.org port 80 (#0)
*   Trying 216.92.116.13...
* connected
* Connected to www.isecom.org (216.92.116.13) port 80 (#0)
> GET / HTTP/1.1
> User-Agent: curl/7.26.0
> Host: www.isecom.org
> Accept: */*
>
* HTTP 1.0, assume close after body
< HTTP/1.0 200 OK
< Date: Tue, 07 Feb 2013 09:29:23 GMT
< Server: Apache/2.2.22
< Last-Modified: Fri, 13 Feb 2013 15:48:14 GMT
< ETag: "3e3a-4bd916679ab80"
< Accept-Ranges: bytes
< Content-Length: 15930
```

```
< Identity: The Institute for Security and Open Methodologies
< P3P: Not supported at this time
< Content-Type: text/html
< Age: 247
< Connection: close
<
<!DOCTYPE html PUBLIC "-//W3C//DTD XHTML 1.0 Transitional//EN"
"http://www.w3.org/TR/xhtml1/DTD/xhtml1-transitional.dtd"[]>
<html xmlns="http://www.w3.org/1999/xhtml" dir="ltr" lang="en-
US" xml:lang="en">
[...]
```

As you can see curl selects automatically the HTTP version 1.1, adds host header, user agent and accept. Which points to an important rule for hackers: know your tools.

Luckily curl is a nice tool can be highly customized using switches.

To see all of them use `curl --help`

Some switches for functions similar to the netcat example above are:

- **-H** to add a header line

- **-X** to select a request method (also known as Command)

- **-d** to add POST data

- **-i** to include protocol headers in the output

- **-s** to enable silent mode, useful for scripting

With curl and some bash scripting you can automate web application testing. Looking for interesting HTTP headers from a server can be automated simply with curl and grep:

```
# curl -siX HEAD http://www.isecom.org/ | grep "Server:"
Server: Apache/2.2.22
```

Exercise

4.31   Expand the script above to request more HTTP headers and potentially useful information.

References and Further Reading

http://www.ietf.org/rfc/rfc1945.txt

http://www.ietf.org/rfc/rfc2616.txt

http://www8.org/w8-papers/5c-protocols/key/key.html

http://netcat.sourceforge.net/

http://curl.haxx.se/

Conclusion to Working with Daemons

The World Wide Web is a whole lot more than the Internet: there are all kinds of services besides just HTTP. FTP, SSH, DNS, DHCP and a whole lot more all offer windows into other people's computers – and yours. Understanding how you connect to these services, whether "through the proper channels" or otherwise, is key to knowing how you or your computer can be attacked – or attack. Just remember the motto: Hack everything, but harm none.

System Identification

Introduction to System Identification

"I think my laptop has a virus," one of my students told me. "Can you take a look at it?"

I took the notebook computer from him, didn't open it, but tilted it every direction, looking closely. "Looks like a computer to me," I said, handing it back to him.

"But something's wrong with it," Aidan insisted. "I went to my friend's house and got on the Internet, and something got into my email and sent messages to all my friends."

"Okay, how do you get to your email? Did you install an application?" I asked.

"No, I do it on the web. I mean Internet."

"You mean in a web browser?" He nodded. "Then that means your email is online, not on your computer. So in this case I'd start with your email account. Have you changed the password?"

"Yeah. They shut down my account until I changed it." He looked down, like there was more to the story, but I didn't press him. My bet was that he'd already been yelled at. A lot.

"Have your friends gotten any more of the messages?" I asked instead.

"No." Staring firmly at his shoes.

"And did you choose a decent password? Not 12345?"

Now he smiled. "It's a really hard one. Nobody's ever gonna get it."

I had my doubts about that, but I nodded. "Okay, then, sounds like you've got it all sorted out."

"No," he insisted. "Why would somebody do that?"

Now I had the fish on the hook. "Why don't you find out. Do you have any of those emails that your friends got?"

"Yeah. A bunch of them. People sent them back to me." Ah: there it was. I'd bet his contact list numbered in the dozens. Or the hundreds. That had to have been fun.

"Then it sounds to me like you need to find out exactly where that link in the email goes."

Cameras flashed behind his eyes. "You mean we can do that?"

"Hah," I laughed. "It means YOU can do it. But I'll show you how."

Aidan stopped. "Is this what you mean by the sheep and the wolf you're always talking about?"

"Yes, exactly that. You can be one or the other. Choose now," I told him.

Suddenly he didn't look so much like a kid. "Wolf," he told me.

* * *

System identification can easily be the most important step of any computer attack or defense. Everything you do afterward depends on the data you gather at this stage. What's the operating system of the host that's attacking you, or that you're defending? Can you – or others – see what applications or services are running? How about the administrator's personal details: are they in plain sight anywhere? These are the questions to ask at this stage. Depending on which side you're on, you might be delighted or horrified at what's easily available if you know where to look.

Knowing how an attack works is cool. Knowing how to protect against it or defeat it is even cooler. Here's where we start digging deep and learning how to identify a system and find its weaknesses – whether it's our own system or someone else's.

We'll be using tools that are publicly available and we'll even show you how to use them. It wouldn't make much sense to show you software but not teach you how to use it. As with any security program, they can be used for good or bad purposes. Our mission is to show you both uses so that you can fix your own security challenges, while protecting against similar attacks.

In this lesson, you'll be following two individuals as one teaches and the other person learns. The teacher doesn't always know what the answer will be so you as the reader will not be spoon-fed information either. Learn to break things and learn how to fix those things you broke. Repeat as necessary.

Pay close attention to attributes used in various programs. A slight change in an upper case to a lower case syntax letter may bring you entirely different data, more-so in different operating systems. These first few lessons are the foundation of networking and how the internet works. Each lesson builds on the previous knowledge so don't be in a hurry, but skipping around the paragraphs and pages is a good way to get familiar with this material before you go back and read in depth. Obviously you don't want to overlook a crucial piece of knowledge.

Identifying a Server

"Okay, Aidan, what did you find out?" I was trying not to grit my teeth with the fear that he'd gone and clicked that stupid link in the email his hacked account had sent out.

"I didn't left-click it," Aidan told me, smiling up like he'd read my mind. "I copied it and pasted it into a plain text file."

"The text you could see? Or the actual link?"

He frowned. "I'm not stupid. I right-clicked and chose 'Copy link location.' Then I pasted it here. Look, link.txt."

"Sorry. Just had to be sure. So okay. Where does it go?"

"This crazy domain. Chewmoogoo.com or something. There's a bunch of other stuff after that too," he said, opening his laptop and showing me the link.

"Oh yeah," I told him. "Now we've got 'em. Now let's see what information we can gather and the tools that can help us collect it. First let's talk about domain names and IP addresses."

Identifying the Owner of a Domain

The first step in identifying a remote system is to look at its host name, domain name or IP address. A **whois** lookup on a domain name turns up a bunch of information:

- The identity of the owner of the domain, usually a full name
- Contact information, which may include street addresses, phone numbers and email addresses
- The DNS servers where the domain is registered, which may also tell you the ISP that serves up the domain
- The IP address of the server, another potential clue to the ISP
- Domain name information, like the date it was created, when it was updated or when it will expire

Keep in mind that there are a lot of different domain name registrars, and not all whois databases contain the information for all domains. You may have to look at more than one whois database to find information about the domain that you are investigating.

Aidan soaked this up instantly. "Okay, what do I do?"

"Here's your assignment," I said.

Exercise

5.1 Get the domain name you're investigating. (If you're not Aidan, use isecom.org.) Try the following command on Linux, Windows and OSX.

```
whois isecom.org
```

   a. Who owns the domain?

   b. When was it created? When will it expire? (Does that expiration present an opportunity?)

   c. When was it last updated?

   d. Who are the different contacts listed?

   e. What are its primary and secondary name servers?

5.2 Now do the same lookup in a browser (for instance, http://www.whois.net -> "sample.com"). Here's the critical question: Does it match what you got from your whois   command? Check at least two whois websites. Try http://whois.domaintools.com; can you find more?).

Identifying the IP Address of a Domain

"So what have you got?" I asked Aidan.

"All this stuff. I pasted it in." He showed me his text file.

"That's good. Keep every single scrap of information. What's the domain IP?"

"This thing, isn't it?" Aidan pointed at a long number.

"Yes. You can get the domain's IP address with a whois command, or you can do a DNS lookup with a **ping** command:

```
ping isecom.org
```

"The first thing you'll see is the domain's IP address."

> If you can capture email from the target, examine the **email headers** (see Lesson 9, Email Security); that will give you the IP address of the originating mail host. You can also use resources like search engines (Lesson 20, Social Engineering) or tools like **Maltego** or **FOCA**. Search on terms like the target organization's name, the domain registration point of contact, telephone numbers and addresses. Each of those can lead you to more information.

"Once you've got an IP – or more than one – you need to find out where it is. IP numbers get assigned to service providers all over the globe in big groups. Find out which group an IP address was issued in (and who has the rights to that group, if you can). That can help you find out what server or service provider the website uses and the real gold for you - what country houses that server," I told Aidan. "Bet it's not this one. So here's what you do next."

Exercises

Now you're going to look at DNS records directly. Another way to find information about a domain and server(s) is to use information in DNS. There are three commands to get started.

5.3 Open a terminal window. Try this command:

```
dig isecom.org
```

Does this command work on your OS? Try it in Windows, Linux and OSX.

5.4 Now try this command:

```
host isecom.org
```

Does this command work on your OS? Try it in Windows, Linux and OSX again.

5.5 Finally try this command:

```
nslookup isecom.org
```

Does this command work on your OS? Once again, try it in Windows, Linux and OSX.

What's the DNS server for your target? Does the organization have a mail server? Does the mail server have the same IP address as the web server? What does this suggest? What else can you learn?

5.6 Once you have the IP address, you can access the records of the various members of the **Number Resource Organization** (http://www.arin.net/, http://www.ripe.net/, or http://www.apnic.net/), to gain insight about how IP addresses are distributed.

 Game On: Slash and Burn

It was a grudge match as far as Jace was concerned. The battle of the century, as she thought of it. No matter how much sweat, blood, pain, physical and intellectual force required, the ambitious teen was prepared to win this fight. She had to win since there was no plan B. Her cocoa colored hair swayed over her eyes like a bullfighter taunting with a red cape. A one last calming deep breath and the network killer was prepared to being.

With her nimble fingers floating over the grinning keyboard, she assessed the situation and took stock of here available resources. Jace had a copy of Nmap already loaded into the computer beast. Ping and Traceroute had already been run so the combative hacker was ready to start slashing away.

Down went the first of a rapid succession of keyboard taps. A machine gun couldn't fire as quickly as Jace did when it came to working the computer commands. Ping, down! Traceroute, down! The IP commands didn't stand a chance against her massive barrage of key pecking. Time to live, down! The bloodshed was horrendous, as bits and bytes tumbled across the monitor in blurs. The CLI seemed to direct the incoming blitz of powerful switches, with attack attributes flanking the main network.

Jace maneuvered her main assault to gain a foothold inside the network. Her scouts performed an intensive reconnaissance of forward deployed firewalls, servers, and routers. This data was compared against Common Vulnerabilities and Exposures (CVE) and cross-referenced with Nmap's own Network Scanning information. Each weakness, every vulnerability, and exploit was examined for tactical advantage and damage assessments. A truce was not an option for Jace. She was winning.

It wasn't over yet, she told herself. In fact, all she had done was captured a small part of the enemies resources but the intelligence was invaluable, nonetheless. Jace suffered little causalities on her end. Fingers and knuckles were a slightly sore. She had a small bruise near her forehead where she banged it against the monitor in frustration. TTLs were killing her.

In the end, battle banners gave up details without the need for interrogation or repeated torture using the "bread-boarding" technique. Raspberry pie was kept in reserve. Jace had enough information on the enemy to perform phase two of the network attack. Next phase required loaded emails and the unintentional insider help.

This was always the scariest part of any battle, obtaining turncoats. Jace needed users on the inside who would be sympathetic to her cause. Now was the time for all good security habits to be broken. Social engineering was the weapon of mass disruption in her arsenal. She would have to craft legitimate emails loaded with Trojan soldiers to penetrate the networks inner walls.

As Jace began constructing each malicious email, she knew that she was on the right side of this confrontation. No matter what it took, no matter how long it took, Jace was determined to know which secret flavor of ice cream the local dairy was working on next.

Game continues...

Identifying Services

"So you saved all that stuff, right?" I grinned but tried not to, because I knew the answer even if my teacherly nature made me ask.

Aidan barely let a sideways glance slip: *bonehead* he was thinking, but he said, "Check it out" and handed me his notebook.

"Lots of info now, isn't there?" I scrolled down through the pages.

"Yeah. I need a better way to keep track of stuff," Aidan said, taking the computer back.

"You sure do. What's your target's IP?" This time I smiled openly.

"Well ... there's about five. Maybe more than that. I'm trying to figure out why, because I can ping some and some I can't."

Good man I thought. Once you've got the IPs for a domain you can start digging into services, and that means running hosts. *Oh fun.*

Ping and Traceroute

"You're starting in the right place. You need to make sure there really are active machines. And you're right; ping is your friend. You did remember to ping the domain name, the IP addresses and the host names, didn't you?"

"Which ones are host names?" Aiden asked.

"They're the ones with letters and a dot before the domain name, like www.isecom.org," I told him.

"I don't see any of those."

"Check out your dig results. You didn't try the other ones. Did you try www.isecom.org and ftp.isecom.org and mail.isecom.org?"

"No...."

"Well, if you get a response, there's something alive at that address. And you're getting through the firewall. And they're letting ICMP through." I opened a CLI and entered a command.

```
C:\>ping isecom.org

Pinging isecom.org [216.92.116.13] with 32 bytes of data:
Reply from 216.92.116.13: bytes=32 time=186ms TTL=56
Reply from 216.92.116.13: bytes=32 time=186ms TTL=56
Reply from 216.92.116.13: bytes=32 time=186ms TTL=56
Reply from 216.92.116.13: bytes=32 time=186ms TTL=56

Ping statistics for 216.92.116.13:
   Packets: Sent = 4, Received = 4, Lost = 0 (0% loss),
Approximate round trip times in milli-seconds:
   Minimum = 186ms, Maximum = 186ms, Average = 186ms
```

"You can get an idea of how far the server is from you, both on the network and physically, by the round trip times. Divide in half, and you can get a feel for the distance to the server. I want you to try another tool, traceroute. It's spelled **tracert** in Windows and **traceroute** in Linux. It'll show you the steps packets take from your computer to your target. Like this," I said, and typed again.

```
C:\>tracert isecom.org
```

"Now, here's what I want you to do."

Exercises

5.7 Use traceroute/tracert to put together all the information you can find about the computers and routers between your computer and your target.

5.8 Computers with similar IP addresses are often part of the same network. Ping a valid website or IP address (for example, ping www.isecom.org or ping 216.92.116.13). If you get a successful response, ping the next IP address. Did you get a response? Try more nearby addresses.

5.9 Use a search engine to find out how to estimate the physical distance to the server if you had to go to it. Look for a tool that can help you map the server to a physical location.

5.10 Look for a Visual Trace Route tool online. There are quite a few sites that provide tools like this. This ought to give you a better visualization of where your traffic is going.

Nmap

"Got all that? Now let me introduce you to my little friend," I said, trying to do a Scarface voice. Aidan looked at me like I had two heads, so I cleared my throat, and, um, finished, "nmap."

"It can be really simple, or you can get really tricky. Run the nmap command with a host name or an IP address, and it'll scan that host. Or use a bunch of switches to do really tricky things. If you ask right, it'll try to tell you the OS of your target. We're going to use the 'scan TCP' option, which is -sT."

```
nmap -sT 216.92.116.13

Starting Nmap 5.51 ( http://nmap.org ) at 2012-05-28 10:58 GTB
Daylight Time
Nmap scan report for 216.92.116.13
Host is up (1.1s latency).
Not shown: 969 closed ports
PORT    STATE SERVICE
25/tcp  open  smtp
80/tcp  open  http
```

```
110/tcp   open pop3
119/tcp   open nntp
135/tcp   open msrpc
139/tcp   open netbios-ssn
143/tcp   open imap
445/tcp   open microsoft-ds
465/tcp   open smtps
554/tcp   open rtsp

Nmap done: 1 IP address (1 host up) scanned in 215.42 seconds
```

It's important to remember that nmap isn't the only tool for doing these scans, and that's a good thing. Different tools can give you different results, and in fact any of them can be deliberately misled.

You can tell nmap, for instance, to guess the operating system – but you should not trust its guess! Verify its theory using other tools.

Banner Grabbing

Aidan was gleeful. "Look what I've got now!" He had text documents and a spreadsheet on his laptop, drawings in a paper notebook and color printouts that had to have cost somebody a fortune in ink cartridges.

"Okay, now you know you've got some live machines, who runs it and roughly where it is. Next you want to know what kind of machine it is: what operating system is it running? What services is it running?" I asked him.

This made him less gleeful. "Um, how do I tell?"

"You don't have to. Get the machine to spill its guts: operating system, services and patch levels. When you're the attacker, that makes your job really easy; all you have to do is look up the exploits for that service, software and version. If you're the defender, you'll want to suppress that information. Or better yet, lie." This made him look thoughtful.

"So what you do next is called **banner grabbing**. Fancy word: it's an **enumeration technique** to get all kinds of information on your target active services and ports. I'm going to show you some more commands. You can use telnet, ftp or netcat to grab the banner.

The banner is that old-school text message you'd get at the command line when you connected to tell you what server program is running. So check it out: when I connect to an anonymous FTP server, I get a banner." I typed into my terminal window:

```
ftp isecom.org

Connected to anon.server.
220 ProFTPD Server (Welcome . . . )
User (anon.server:(none)):
```

"That number 220 is a code that says the server's ready for a new user. And isn't this nice: ProFTPD Server is the FTP program running on that host. Now we hit the web to find out what OS ProFTPD runs on, what it can do ... what's messed up, if anything." I rattled away on the keyboard. "Here: your next assignment is to use the ftp command."

Exercises

5.11 You can use FTP with either a host name or an IP address, like this:

```
ftp isecom.org
```
or
```
ftp 216.92.116.13
```

Try both to see what banner the FTP server returns. Your result may look like this:

```
Connected to isecom.org.
220 ftp316.pair.com NcFTPd Server (licensed copy) ready.
User (isecom.org:(none)):
```

5.12 You can use Telnet with either a host name or an IP address, too. With either one you can specify the port, which is 21 when we're connecting to FTP:

```
telnet isecom.org 21
```
or

```
telnet 216.92.116.13 21
```

Again, see what banner the server returns – if anything. You may get something like this:

```
220 ftp316.pair.com NcFTPd Server (licensed copy) ready.
```

5.13 Use netcat with either a host name or an IP address, too. Just like with Telnet, you can specify the port, which is 21 for FTP:

```
nc isecom.org 21
```

or

```
nc 216.92.116.13 21
```

Again, see what banner the server returns – if anything.

Misleading Banners

"Here's the trick," I told Aidan. "You can change the banner. That's one kind of **spoofing** – lying about who you are. So I can change my banner to read *NoneOfYourBusiness Server*, which is cute, but a Unix system with a banner that reads *WS_FTP Server* is going to throw people off, because that's a Windows FTP server."

"Wait a minute – how do you change the banner?" he asked.

"Glad you asked," I said.

Exercise

5.14 Get on the web and find out how to change the banners for SMTP, FTP, SSH, HTTP and HTTPS. Is it hard to do? In other words, should you just trust what banners say?

Automated Banner Grabbing

"Now check this out. We can go back to nmap and automate this; we have to use the -sTV switches to get banners." I typed the first line and got this report:

```
nmap -sTV -Pn -n --top-ports 10 --reason -oA hhs_5_06
hackerhighschool.org


Starting Nmap 6.00 ( http://nmap.org ) at 2012-06-23 05:10 CEST

Nmap scan report for hackerhighschool.org (216.92.116.13)

Host is up, received user-set (0.30s latency).

PORT     STATE   SERVICE    REASON      VERSION
21/tcp   open    ftp        syn-ack     NcFTPd
22/tcp   open    ssh        syn-ack     OpenSSH 5.9 (protocol 2.0)
23/tcp   closed  telnet     conn-refused
25/tcp   filtered smtp      no-response
80/tcp   open    http       syn-ack     Apache httpd 2.2.22
110/tcp  open    pop3       syn-ack     Dovecot pop3d
139/tcp  closed  netbios-ssn conn-refused
443/tcp  open    ssl/http   syn-ack     Apache httpd 2.2.22
445/tcp  closed  microsoft-ds conn-refused
3389/tcp closed  ms-wbt-server conn-refused
Service Info: OS: Unix


Service detection performed. Please report any incorrect results at
http://nmap.org/submit/ .

Nmap done: 1 IP address (1 host up) scanned in 17.32 seconds
```

"Nmap found NcFTPd, OpenSSH 5.9 (protocol 2.0) and Apache httpd 2.2.22. Bingo: the OS is Unix. Sometimes the banners give you the operating system version, but we're going to need a little bit more info to get specific," I continued. "Here's what I want you to do."

Exercises

5.15 Use nmap on your target (hackerhighschool.org, if you're not Aidan).

5.16 Try it again with the option --**version-intensity number** using numbers from 0 to 9 to get more accurate results. What differences can you see in these reports?

Identifying Services from Ports and Protocols

"Nmap did that last scan by looking for default services. But you can do it from the other direction too: look for open ports first, then see what service is actually behind them," I said.

"Wait a minute," Aidan demanded. "Aren't the ports always the same?"

"Yeah, in theory they are. But really, port numbers are sort of a gentlemen's agreement. I can put my services on different ports if I want."

"Okay, how do I do that?"

"Start by looking at your own local computer. Go to a command line and run the **netstat** command with the **-a** switch to scan all ports. Like this," I demonstrated.

```
netstat -a
```

The young hacker followed my example, then burst out, "Whoa! All of these are open?"

I looked at his screen. "Your computer is named Quasimodo?"

```
Active Connections
Proto  Local Address            Foreign Address          State
TCP    Quasimodo:microsoft-ds   Quasimodo:0              LISTENING
TCP    Quasimodo:1025           Quasimodo:0              LISTENING
TCP    Quasimodo:1030           Quasimodo:0              LISTENING
TCP    Quasimodo:5000           Quasimodo:0              LISTENING
TCP    Quasimodo:netbios-ssn    Quasimodo:0              LISTENING
TCP    Quasimodo:1110           216.239.57.147:httpTIME_WAIT
```

```
UDP     Quasimodo:microsoft-ds    *:*
UDP     Quasimodo:isakmp          *:*
UDP     Quasimodo:1027            *:*
UDP     Quasimodo:1034            *:*
UDP     Quasimodo:1036            *:*
UDP     Quasimodo:ntp             *:*
UDP     Quasimodo:netbios-ns      *:*
UDP     Quasimodo:netbios-dgm     *:*
```

"Yeah, Quasimodo," Aidan grinned. "The Hunchback."

"Okay then, Victor. Here's what I want you to do."

Exercises

5.17 Run netstat on your local computer, using the -a switch.

```
netstat -a
```

Which ports are open?

5.18 Run netstat on your local computer, using the -o switch.

```
netstat -o
```

What services are listening behind the open ports?

5.19 Run netstat on your local computer, using the -aon switch combination.

```
netstat -aon
```

What does this combination get you?

5.20 Using a web search engine, match these ports with the services that run on them. Some of them you need for things like networking. But do you really want all the services you see running?

5.21 Run nmap, using the -sS (to do a SYN or so-called "stealth" scan) and -O (for guess operating system) switches and the IP address 127.0.0.1 as the target. The IP address 127.0.0.1 is called the **loopback** address. It always means localhost, your local computer.

```
nmap -sS -O 127.0.0.1
```

a. What open ports does nmap find? What services and programs are using these ports?

b. Now try running nmap while you have a web browser or telnet client open. How does this change the results?

The "stealth" scan uses just the first part of the TCP three-way handshake – the SYN packet – to probe a port without fully setting up a connection. While this gets you past the system's logs (which won't log your probe unless you really make a connection), it is NOT undetectable. Any intrusion detection system is going to see your big, greasy fingerprints all over the network, so don't fool yourself that you're really being stealthy.

5.22 Nmap has additional command line switches. What do -sV, -sU, -sP, -A, --top-ports and --reason do? What other possibilities are there? If you were an attacker and you wanted to remain stealthy rather than banging on the server, which switches should you *not* use, or use?

5.23 Go to www.foundstone.com, and find, download and install **fport** on your Windows box. It's similar to netstat, but it also details which programs are using the open ports and protocols. Run it. How does it compare to netstat?

System Fingerprinting

"You didn't go stumbling around and ringing bells, did you?" I asked.

Aidan replied slowly, really thinking about it, "No, I don't think so. But does it really matter? I mean their servers are way over in …."

I interrupted. "I don't know where they are, I don't care, you're going to operate ethically – and carefully – as long as you're working with me."

"Okay," sheepishly.

"It's a good policy to leave no tracks. Which is almost impossible. But you should always be trying. Because tracks are exactly what you're going to work on next. Or actually, fingerprints…."

"Hey! Those aren't the same!"

"Okay, got me. But regardless, we're going to put everything together to **fingerprint** your target, find the OS and all its services."

Scanning Remote Computers

"What did you finally get back on your stealth scans?" I asked. Aidan showed me a report he'd pasted into a text document.

```
nmap -sS -O 216.92.116.13
```

```
Starting Nmap 5.51 ( http://nmap.org ) at 2012-05-28 16:54 GTB
Daylight Time
Nmap scan report for isecom.org (216.92.116.13)
Host is up (0.19s latency).
Not shown: 965 closed ports

PORT     STATE    SERVICE
21/tcp   open     ftp
22/tcp   open     ssh
25/tcp   filtered smtp
26/tcp   open     rsftp
80/tcp   open     http
110/tcp  open     pop3
111/tcp  filtered rpcbind
113/tcp  filtered auth
135/tcp  filtered msrpc
139/tcp  filtered netbios-ssn
143/tcp  open     imap
161/tcp  filtered snmp
179/tcp  filtered bgp
306/tcp  open     unknown
443/tcp  open     https
445/tcp  filtered microsoft-ds
465/tcp  open     smtps
514/tcp  filtered shell
543/tcp  open     klogin
544/tcp  open     kshell
587/tcp  open     submission
646/tcp  filtered ldp
800/tcp  filtered mdbs_daemon
993/tcp  open     imaps
995/tcp  open     pop3s
1720/tcp filtered H.323/Q.931
2105/tcp open     eklogin
6667/tcp filtered irc
7000/tcp filtered afs3-fileserver
7001/tcp filtered afs3-callback
7007/tcp filtered afs3-bos
7777/tcp filtered cbt
9000/tcp filtered cslistener
12345/tcp filtered netbus
31337/tcp filtered Elite
Device type: general purpose|storage-misc
Running (JUST GUESSING): FreeBSD 7.X|6.X (88%)
```

```
Aggressive OS guesses: FreeBSD 7.0-BETA4 - 7.0 (88%), FreeBSD 7.0-
RC1 (88%), FreeBSD 7.0-RELEASE - 8.0-STABLE (88%), FreeBSD 7.0-
STABLE (88%), FreeBSD
 7.1-RELEASE (88%), FreeBSD 6.3-RELEASE (86%), FreeNAS 0.7 (FreeBSD
7.2-RELEASE) (85%)
No exact OS matches for host (test conditions non-ideal).
Network Distance: 8 hops
OS detection performed. Please report any incorrect results at
http://nmap.org/submit/ .
Nmap done: 1 IP address (1 host up) scanned in 24.09 seconds
```

"See all those ports marked **filtered**? That means no packets came back so NMAP assumes they're being filtered by a firewall. But the truth is we don't really know why since the packets didn't return to tell us anything. But in this case they probably are being filtered by a firewall because they're well-known and vulnerable ports that should always be blocked. But look: ports 21, 22 and 80 – that's FTP, Secure Shell and HTTP – are all open." I looked over at Aidan.

"Sheep?" he asked hopefully.

"Well, rightful prey, at least. Okay. The last thing that nmap does is try to figure out the operating system on your target. Lots of the time, like now, it only makes an 'aggressive guess,' but that's usually pretty good. Since the scan shows FTP and SSH open, the banners you grabbed would be the next piece of evidence.

"Hit the web, it tells us NcFTPd is a Unix program and that FreeBSD is a Unix-type operating system. SSH you'd usually find on Unix-like OSs. So it's likely the server's running some version of FreeBSD. You know those banners can be spoofed, but it's a reasonable guess.

"Now, depending on where your target is, your next step might be to find the ISP. The ISP itself might be famous for hosting spammers or malicious sites – do a search – but you might be able to whine to them and get your evil attacker shut down. In your case I think it's not going to be an ISP you can really deal with....

"Because it's in..." Aidan burst in, but I held up my finger.

"Stop. Your information is your information. I don't need it, as long as you are being ethical and safe. Which you are."

Aidan nodded.

"So watcha gonna do?" I asked.

"Well, they've got a web server running, right?" Aidan began, and all I could do was smile.

 Game On: Hacking for Nutmeg

Sweet G and Jace had treated themselves to ice cream they bought at the dairy. Since G was allergic to nutmeg, they were both leery about a new flavor called "Rum Raisin." Raisins were a weakness for the two ladies since they both loved anything with raisins. Grandma would buy a box of raisins one day and the next day the box would be empty. "They just vanished into thin air, G," Jace would explain with bits of raisins stuck in her teeth. Rum Raisin sounded so good but they checked the label to see if nutmeg was an ingredient. Just to be extra sure, Jace interrogated the dairy clerk.

Kople, the clerk, could see that these two women meant business so he called his manager to be extra-extra sure. "No ma'am, no nutmeg in the Rum Raisin," he said with slight fear in his voice and sweat on his upper lip.

Back at the apartment when Sweet G's tongue began to swell, they both knew that nutmeg was in the ice cream. Grandma kind of laughed about it and she talked funny but Jace didn't think the betrayal was humorous at all. The teen didn't like being lied to so she waited for G to go to bed before she started her evening's work.

The latest versions of Metasploit have Nmap built into the network framework. Jace didn't want to waste too much time since she decided the target wasn't using too many security features. Her target was the local dairy; what would they want to secure? Maybe the cows?

To check how vulnerable that network was, she performed an Nmap full TCP connect scan. This type of port scan isn't stealthy but provides a good way to check each port on the target network. The slower the scan, the better chance of staying hidden. Quick scans would show up in audit logs due to the high volume of traffic Nmap is requesting. The full connect scan not only sends a SYN packet to each port, it waits for a SYN ACK indicating an open port, completes the session by sending an ACK, then quickly sends a reset (RST) command back to the port to terminate the session. If a port doesn't report its status it can mean that the port is behind the firewall, the server is switched off, the response got lost on the Internet or any number of things. All you really know for sure is that you didn't receive a response, but you can't always know the reason for sure.

Nmap did tell Jace the port state of each port on the target and the MAC address of that device. She wanted to scan a range of target addresses so she typed in

```
nmap -sT - sV 172.16.*.*
```

The asterisk is a wild card switch for scanning multiple targets. She could have used other IP range wildcards like 172.16.0-255.0-255 or even 172.16.0.0/16.

When Nmap returned the results, she then turned to Metasploit's internal vulnerability scanners. The hacker did this by typing db_autopwn –p –t –e. Metasploit used the information from Nmap to search that target for vulnerabilities that Metasploit already knew about within its own database. "That was easy," Jace said as she cracked her knuckles.

Jace had pulled an all-nighter to get inside thatparticular network. Sleep deprivation was about to pay off. "BINGO," she said aloud as the monitor sprewd out data.

Then the crash. 404 file not found. Connection terminated.

She was so mad. Mad enough to burst out of her skin and mangle the computer. Jace stopped breathing while her eyes narrowed. Nostrils opened wide as her body went into attack mode. Fight or Flight? Jace was positioned and postured to fight.

The only question was, "who or what was she going to fight."

Fingernails gouged into her hardened palms, fists stone hard. With automatic eyes, she gathered intel on her surroundings. Just as Jace started to leap down onto the machine, Sweet G slide the bedroom light switch on. Darkness shattered into sudden light.

Jace didn't move, didn't blink, didn't breathe. Grandma slightly entered Jace's bedroom with concern and curiosity. "Honey, you alright? I heard you shout and it," grandma said before switching gears. Jace turned to face the doorway, to face Sweet G.

"You look terrible," the elder said. Jace's lit fuse was snuffed out by her grandmothers presence. Jace phased back to reality, took a slow breathe to bring color back into her tense body. "I'm sorry Sweet G. I didn't mean to wake you." She fingered her rough hair to one side, knowing how bad she must look at the moment.

Grandma kept her distance even though she wanted to hug Jace and comfort her. Grandma didn't have her glasses on but she could sense frustration and terrible anger. "What's going on that you need to spend the entire night working on," G asked.

"Grandma, I appreciate your concern but it's nothing that you would understand," Jace appeared sympathetic as oxygen returned to her slumped body. "Oh really! Try me," G said now with arms folded. Grandma approached the unused bed and sat down across from Jace in a defiant manner. "Bring it on," her composure said.

"Look here Ms. Jace. My contract says that I am supposed to act concerned for your well-being and pretend to care when you need help," Sweet G said. "What contract," Jace replied. "Well, my grandmother's contract. Every grandma out there has a contract. Just like moms and dads. We all have contracts that say what we are supposed to do and mine says that I am required to act concerned. So 'fess up little lady," G announced in a business manner. Jace smiled for the first time in twelve hours.

"Well, I'm trying to get inside a network. One of the first things I do is find out what type of operating system the network is using," Jace said. "I use several different programs to try to determine which operating system is being used. My favorite is Nmap," Grandma nodded while Jace continued. "Once I know which operating system is on that network, I can look up to see if there are holes in the platform," the teen said expecting Sweet G to drop the issue since the talk would be too technical for her to understand.

Instead, her grandmother continued to look interested and focused on Jace. G said, "Why do you want to get into this network? I'm sorry, I didn't mean to interrupt you. But continue anyways." Jace was off-balance by the question. "Well, I'm trying to get inside the network because I want to know some very important information. I need to know something that is very special," Jace replied. Grandma said, "Like what."

Jace sucked in a lung full of air and decided there was no danger if she told the truth to Sweet G. She probably didn't understand any of this hacking stuff anyways, Jace thought. "I think Oma's Dairy is putting nutmeg in their new flavor of ice cream. It's a secret that they have kept real quiet but I want to know why they aren't telling anyone," the teen explained.

Sweet G stood up from the bed and started walking to the bedroom doorway. "Yes, they put nutmeg in Rum Raisin," G said as she approached the door.

Jace said, "What?!"

Grandma repeated herself, "Nutmeg, they admitted it."

Now Jace was really thrown off-balance as she raced towards her grandmother before she could leave the bedroom. "How do you know? Even the clerk told us there wasn't any nutmeg in it. Nobody knew that, except for you and your overstuffed tongue," the puzzled teen rebutted.

Sweet G continued towards her own bedroom and said," They announced it on TV last night. It was a simple labeling mistake. The dairy is offering a free sundae to anyone who was bothered by the mistake. I'm going to ask for extra cherries on my free sundae."

Game Over

Feed Your Head: Going Deep with Nmap

Say you've identified the hostname, the owner, the network and verified the host is up. Now in order to identify a system you need to find some open ports. Don't forget that the host can be up but have all ports closed (or even filtered).

You can use the famous Network Mapper (aka **nmap**) tool from Fyodor to do this task. Nmap is a port scanner and is able to remotely probe computers for open ports and related network services. When you execute nmap, depending on the command line switches that you use, you'll get a list of open ports and the services or protocols that use those ports. Nmap may also be able to determine what operating system your computer is using.

Nmap has many options and scan types. We will use a few nmap options but you can always use

```
nmap --help
```
or
```
man nmap
```
to see the details.

Before we begin, have you read Lesson 3? No? Now's the time to do it! Back already? No? Then go now!

Ok, explain the differences between TCP and UDP and describe the three-way handshake. Knowing how this works is important for understanding how nmap works.

Nmap syntax is:

```
nmap scan-techniques host-discovery options target
```

- **scan-techniques** specify what kind of packets will be used and how responses from target should be interpreted. The main available techniques are:

    ◦ **-sS** SYN scan (yes, only the first part of thee-handshake)

    ◦ **-sT** TCP Connect scan (full three-way handshake)

    ◦ **-sA** ACK scan (send only ACK packets)

    ◦ **-sU** UDP Scan

- o **-O** OS Detection

- o **-A** All functionalities such as OS detection, plugins, traceroute

- **host-discovery** specifies the techniques used to define if a host is alive or not. If the host is alive it will be scanned, otherwise not.

  - o **-PE** check if host responds to a ping

  - o **-PS** check if host responds to a SYN

  - o **-PA** check if host responds to an ACK

  - o **-PU** check if host responds to a UDP datagram

  - o **-PN** don't check, treat all hosts as active (we'll use this because we know that our target is alive, since we checked earlier)

- **options** specify further details for the selected scan type, such as

  - o **-p1-65535** port numbers to scan (in this example from 1 to 65535).

  - o **--top-ports <number>** nmap knows which are the most frequently used ports, and can scan only for the top <number> specified

  - o **-T0, -T1, -T2, -T3, -T4** for the scan speed, where 0 is slow and 4 is fast (slower means more stealthy and with less network congestion)

  - o **-oA <filename>** for the output in all three main nmap formats (we will always use it to keep track of our activities)

  - o **--reason** nmap writes about its interpreted results (recommended)

  - o **--packet-trace** similar to –reason but you will see the traffic traces (you use these to learn about a scan technique and to troubleshoot scans)

  - o **-n** do not resolve DNS (we will not use DNS because we have already analyzed it manually)

TCP Scan

Our first scan starts with the following command:

```
nmap -sT -Pn -n --top-ports 10 -oA hhs_5_tcp hackerhighschool.org
```

Which gives us this output:

```
Starting Nmap 6.00 ( http://nmap.org ) at 2012-06-23 04:10 CEST
Nmap scan report for hackerhighschool.org (216.92.116.13)
Host is up (0.23s latency).
PORT     STATE   SERVICE
21/tcp   open    ftp
22/tcp   open    ssh
23/tcp   closed  telnet
25/tcp   filtered smtp
80/tcp   open    http
110/tcp  open    pop3
139/tcp  closed  netbios-ssn
443/tcp  open    https
445/tcp  closed  microsoft-ds
3389/tcp closed  ms-wbt-server

Nmap done: 1 IP address (1 host up) scanned in 2.04 seconds
```

We found some ports open, some closed and one filtered. What does this mean? It depends on the scan type (in this case -sT). And we can use the --reason option to see why nmap has inferred a particular State.

```
nmap  -sT  -Pn  -n  --top-ports  10  --reason  -oA  hhs_5_tcp_02
hackerhighschool.org

Starting Nmap 6.00 ( http://nmap.org ) at 2012-06-23 04:17 CEST
Nmap scan report for hackerhighschool.org (216.92.116.13)
Host is up, received user-set (0.22s latency).
PORT     STATE    SERVICE       REASON
21/tcp   open     ftp           syn-ack
22/tcp   open     ssh           syn-ack
23/tcp   closed   telnet        conn-refused
25/tcp   filtered smtp          no-response
80/tcp   open     http          syn-ack
110/tcp  open     pop3          syn-ack
139/tcp  closed   netbios-ssn   conn-refused
443/tcp  open     https         syn-ack
445/tcp  closed   microsoft-ds  conn-refused
3389/tcp closed   ms-wbt-server conn-refused

Nmap done: 1 IP address (1 host up) scanned in 2.26 seconds
```

Now we know how nmap "maps" replies to states for **TCP Scan**:

- **open**: target replies with a SYN ACK packet

- **closed**: TCP connection refused

- **filtered**: no reply from target

When you find open and filtered ports use other scan techniques to find out exactly why.

SYN Scan

Another famous scanning technique is the SYN scan. When it's doing this type of scan, nmap sends only a SYN packet without completing the three-way handshake. This is also called a "half-open" or "stealth" scan because there TCP connections are not completed. (Be very clear that while a target may not log a connection, you are still making digital "noise" that can be detected.) Use the -sS scan type as follows:

```
nmap   -sS   -Pn   -n   --top-ports   10   --reason   -oA   hhs_5_syn
hackerhighschool.org

Starting Nmap 6.00 ( http://nmap.org ) at 2012-06-24 12:58 CEST
Nmap scan report for hackerhighschool.org (216.92.116.13)
Host is up, received user-set (0.15s latency).
PORT      STATE    SERVICE      REASON
21/tcp    open     ftp          syn-ack
22/tcp    open     ssh          syn-ack
23/tcp    closed   telnet       reset
25/tcp    filtered smtp         no-response
80/tcp    open     http         syn-ack
110/tcp   open     pop3         syn-ack
139/tcp   filtered netbios-ssn  no-response
443/tcp   open     https        syn-ack
445/tcp   filtered microsoft-ds no-response
3389/tcp  closed   ms-wbt-server reset

Nmap done: 1 IP address (1 host up) scanned in 1.81 seconds
```

The results are similar to the TCP Scan but notice the differences between "full" TCP Scan and "half-open" SYN scan, comparing the results (with –reason and –packet-trace) using the same target with -sT, -sS and -sA (ACK scan).

UDP scan

Another scan technique is the UDP scan (-sU): knowing the reason is fundamental to getting good results.

```
nmap  -sU  -Pn  -n  --top-ports  10  --reason  -oA  hhs_5_udp
hackerhighschool.org

Starting Nmap 6.00 ( http://nmap.org ) at 2012-06-23 04:28 CEST
Nmap scan report for hackerhighschool.org (216.92.116.13)
Host is up, received user-set (0.23s latency).
PORT     STATE        SERVICE    REASON
53/udp   closed       domain     port-unreach
67/udp   open|filtered dhcps     no-response
123/udp  closed       ntp        port-unreach
135/udp  closed       msrpc      port-unreach
137/udp  closed       netbios-ns port-unreach
138/udp  closed       netbios-dgm port-unreach
161/udp  closed       snmp       port-unreach
445/udp  closed       microsoft-ds port-unreach
631/udp  closed       ipp        port-unreach
1434/udp closed       ms-sql-m   port-unreach

Nmap done: 1 IP address (1 host up) scanned in 2.05 seconds
```

It can be a little bit confusing. What happened? We see some of the reasons: port-unreach (unreachable, i.e. closed) and no-response (open|filtered). Why? We need more details. We can use the packet trace option and limit the scan to two ports, for example ports 53 and 67 UDP:

```
nmap -sU -Pn -n -p53,67 --reason --packet-trace -oA hhs_5_udp_02
hackerhighschool.org

Starting Nmap 6.00 ( http://nmap.org ) at 2012-06-23 04:32 CEST
SENT  (0.0508s)  UDP  192.168.100.53:54940  >  216.92.116.13:67
ttl=46 id=54177 iplen=28
SENT  (0.0509s)  UDP  192.168.100.53:54940  >  216.92.116.13:53
ttl=37 id=17751 iplen=40
RCVD  (0.3583s)  ICMP  216.92.116.13  >  192.168.100.53  Port
unreachable (type=3/code=3) ttl=54 id=1724 iplen=56
SENT  (2.5989s)  UDP  192.168.100.53:54941  >  216.92.116.13:67
ttl=49 id=33695 iplen=28
Nmap scan report for hackerhighschool.org (216.92.116.13)
Host is up, received user-set (0.31s latency).
PORT    STATE        SERVICE REASON
53/udp  closed       domain port-unreach
```

```
67/udp open|filtered dhcps  no-response

Nmap done: 1 IP address (1 host up) scanned in 4.15 seconds
```

We found out that 192.168.100.53 sent UDP packets to port 53 and 67 of hackerhighschool.org. What happened here? Port 67 is unresponsive and for 53 we received a Port Unreachable (T03C03).

Port Unreachable means the port is closed, and as for no-response – even if is a normal response for UDP – we don't know if the service is active or not because the UDP protocol can only reply if it receives the correct packets. Can we investigate it more? Yes, using the -sV Service Scan in which nmap tries to send well-known packets for UDP services.

Service Scan (UDP)

```
nmap    -sUV   -Pn   -n   -p53,67   --reason   --packet-trace   -oA
hhs_5_udp_03 hackerhighschool.org

Starting Nmap 6.00 ( http://nmap.org ) at 2012-06-23 04:44 CEST
SENT   (0.1730s)   UDP   192.168.100.53:62664   >   216.92.116.13:53
ttl=48 id=23048 iplen=40
SENT   (0.1731s)   UDP   192.168.100.53:62664   >   216.92.116.13:67
ttl=48 id=53183 iplen=28
RCVD   (0.4227s)   ICMP   216.92.116.13   >   192.168.100.53   Port
unreachable (type=3/code=3) ttl=54 id=20172 iplen=56
SENT   (2.4252s)   UDP   192.168.100.53:62665   >   216.92.116.13:67
ttl=50 id=39909 iplen=28
NSOCK   (3.8460s)   UDP   connection   requested   to   216.92.116.13:67
(IOD #1) EID 8
NSOCK   (3.8460s)   Callback:   CONNECT   SUCCESS   for   EID   8
[216.92.116.13:67]
Service scan sending probe RPCCheck to 216.92.116.13:67 (udp)
...and 80 more packets...
Nmap scan report for hackerhighschool.org (216.92.116.13)
Host is up, received user-set (0.25s latency).
PORT   STATE       SERVICE REASON     VERSION
53/udp closed      domain port-unreach
67/udp open|filtered dhcps  no-response
```

We're not lucky this time, since we got the same results. A good hacker can also try specific UDP packets manually, or with the proper client on the standard port 67. We have already used the service scan, the next step for service identification. Learn the well known services on your local machine and do some exercises, then continue with banner grabbing.

Exercises

5.24 Go to http://nmap.org, download and install the latest version of nmap for your operating system.

5.25 Repeat all the scans in this section using more ports. Have in mind that you need the sudo command on Linux systems, or local administrator rights on Windows.

5.26 Create a table reference for all scan techniques mapping state, reason and the real response from the target (packet-trace).

OS Detection

Knowing services is important to fingerprinting the target machine. Nmap can help again using more options such as -A for all scans and -O for OS detection, using the default ports:

```
sudo nmap -A -Pn -n --reason -oA hhs_5_all hackerhighschool.org

Starting Nmap 6.00 ( http://nmap.org ) at 2012-06-23 05:38 CEST
Nmap scan report for hackerhighschool.org (216.92.116.13)
Host is up, received user-set (0.21s latency).
Not shown: 971 closed ports
Reason: 971 resets
PORT     STATE    SERVICE       REASON      VERSION
21/tcp   open     ftp           syn-ack     NcFTPd
22/tcp   open     ssh           syn-ack     OpenSSH 5.9 (protocol 2.0)
|                               ssh-hostkey:                    1024
cd:27:c2:bf:ad:35:e5:67:e0:1b:cf:ef:ac:2b:18:9a (DSA)
|_1024 17:83:c5:8a:7a:ac:6c:90:48:04:0b:e5:9c:e5:4d:ab (RSA)
25/tcp   filtered smtp          no-response
26/tcp   open     tcpwrapped    syn-ack
80/tcp   open     http          syn-ack     Apache httpd 2.2.22
|_http-title: Hacker Highschool - Security Awareness for Teens
110/tcp  open     pop3          syn-ack     Dovecot pop3d
|_pop3-capabilities: USER  CAPA  UIDL  TOP  OK(K)  RESP-CODES
PIPELINING STLS SASL(PLAIN LOGIN)
```

```
111/tcp  filtered rpcbind      no-response
113/tcp  open    tcpwrapped   syn-ack
143/tcp  open    imap         syn-ack   Dovecot imapd
|_imap-capabilities: LOGIN-REFERRALS  QUOTA  AUTH=PLAIN  LIST-
STATUS  CHILDREN  CONTEXT=SEARCH  THREAD=REFERENCES  UIDPLUS  SORT
IDLE   MULTIAPPEND   CONDSTORE   ESEARCH   Capability   UNSELECT
AUTH=LOGINA0001  IMAP4rev1   ID   WITHIN   QRESYNC  LIST-EXTENDED
SORT=DISPLAY THREAD=REFS STARTTLS OK completed SEARCHRES ENABLE
I18NLEVEL=1 LITERAL+ ESORT SASL-IR NAMESPACE
161/tcp  filtered snmp         no-response
179/tcp  filtered bgp          no-response
306/tcp  open    tcpwrapped   syn-ack
443/tcp  open    ssl/http     syn-ack   Apache httpd 2.2.22
|                    ssl-cert:                    Subject:
commonName=www.isecom.org/organizationName=ISECOM    -    The
Institute       for       Security       and       Open
Methodologies/stateOrProvinceName=New York/countryName=US
| Not valid before: 2010-12-11 00:00:00
|_Not valid after: 2013-12-10 23:59:59
|_http-title: Site doesn't have a title (text/html).
|_sslv2: server supports SSLv2 protocol, but no SSLv2 cyphers
465/tcp  open    ssl/smtp     syn-ack   Postfix smtpd
|_smtp-commands: kunatri.pair.com, PIPELINING, SIZE 41943040,
ETRN, AUTH PLAIN LOGIN, AUTH=PLAIN LOGIN, ENHANCEDSTATUSCODES,
8BITMIME, DSN,
| ssl-cert: Subject: commonName=*.pair.com/organizationName=pair
Networks, Inc./stateOrProvinceName=Pennsylvania/countryName=US
| Not valid before: 2012-01-10 00:00:00
|_Not valid after: 2015-01-09 23:59:59
543/tcp  open    tcpwrapped   syn-ack
544/tcp  open    tcpwrapped   syn-ack
587/tcp  open    smtp         syn-ack   Postfix smtpd
|_smtp-commands: kunatri.pair.com, PIPELINING, SIZE 41943040,
ETRN, STARTTLS, ENHANCEDSTATUSCODES, 8BITMIME, DSN,
| ssl-cert: Subject: commonName=*.pair.com/organizationName=pair
Networks, Inc./stateOrProvinceName=Pennsylvania/countryName=US
| Not valid before: 2012-01-10 00:00:00
|_Not valid after: 2015-01-09 23:59:59
646/tcp  filtered ldp          no-response
800/tcp  filtered mdbs_daemon   no-response
993/tcp  open    ssl/imap     syn-ack   Dovecot imapd
| ssl-cert: Subject: commonName=*.pair.com/organizationName=pair
Networks, Inc./stateOrProvinceName=Pennsylvania/countryName=US
| Not valid before: 2012-01-10 00:00:00
|_Not valid after: 2015-01-09 23:59:59
```

```
|_sslv2: server supports SSLv2 protocol, but no SSLv2 cyphers
|_imap-capabilities: LOGIN-REFERRALS completed OK SORT=DISPLAY
Capability UNSELECT AUTH=PLAIN AUTH=LOGINA0001 IMAP4rev1 QUOTA
CONDSTORE LIST-STATUS ID SEARCHRES WITHIN CHILDREN LIST-EXTENDED
ESORT     ESEARCH     QRESYNC     CONTEXT=SEARCH     THREAD=REFS
THREAD=REFERENCES  I18NLEVEL=1  UIDPLUS  NAMESPACE  ENABLE  SORT
LITERAL+ IDLE SASL-IR MULTIAPPEND
995/tcp  open   ssl/pop3    syn-ack   Dovecot pop3d
|_sslv2: server supports SSLv2 protocol, but no SSLv2 cyphers
|_pop3-capabilities: OK(K) CAPA RESP-CODES UIDL PIPELINING USER
TOP SASL(PLAIN LOGIN)
| ssl-cert: Subject: commonName=*.pair.com/organizationName=pair
Networks, Inc./stateOrProvinceName=Pennsylvania/countryName=US
| Not valid before: 2012-01-10 00:00:00
|_Not valid after: 2015-01-09 23:59:59
2105/tcp open   tcpwrapped   syn-ack
6667/tcp filtered irc          no-response
7000/tcp filtered afs3-fileserver no-response
7001/tcp filtered afs3-callback  no-response
7007/tcp filtered afs3-bos      no-response
7777/tcp filtered cbt          no-response
9000/tcp filtered cslistener    no-response
31337/tcp filtered Elite        no-response
Device type: general purpose|firewall|specialized|router
Running  (JUST  GUESSING):  FreeBSD  6.X|7.X|8.X  (98%),  m0n0wall
FreeBSD  6.X  (91%),  OpenBSD  4.X  (91%),  VMware  ESX  Server  4.X
(90%),  AVtech embedded (89%),  Juniper JUNOS 9.X (89%)
OS  CPE:  cpe:/o:freebsd:freebsd:6.3  cpe:/o:freebsd:freebsd:7.0
cpe:/o:freebsd:freebsd:8.1             cpe:/o:m0n0wall:freebsd
cpe:/o:openbsd:openbsd:4.0             cpe:/o:vmware:esxi:4.1
cpe:/o:m0n0wall:freebsd:6 cpe:/o:juniper:junos:9
Aggressive OS guesses: FreeBSD 6.3-RELEASE (98%), FreeBSD 7.0-
RELEASE (95%), FreeBSD 8.1-RELEASE (94%), FreeBSD 7.1-PRERELEASE
7.2-STABLE  (94%),  FreeBSD  7.0-RELEASE  -  8.0-STABLE  (92%),
FreeBSD  7.1-RELEASE  (92%),  FreeBSD  7.2-RELEASE  -  8.0-RELEASE
(91%),  FreeBSD 7.0-RC1 (91%),  FreeBSD 7.0-STABLE (91%),  m0n0wall
1.3b11 - 1.3b15 FreeBSD-based firewall (91%)
No exact OS matches for host (test conditions non-ideal).
Network Distance: 12 hops
Service Info: Host: kunatri.pair.com; OS: Unix

TRACEROUTE (using port 1723/tcp)
HOP RTT     ADDRESS
[...]
8  94.98 ms 89.221.34.153
```

```
 9  93.70 ms 89.221.34.110
10 211.60 ms 64.210.21.150
11 ...
12 209.28 ms 216.92.116.13

OS and Service detection performed. Please report any incorrect
results at http://nmap.org/submit/ .
Nmap done: 1 IP address (1 host up) scanned in 57.94 seconds
```

Using -A is possible to see more data. Specialized plugins fetch more information from a server, perform OS Guessing and use a variant of traceroute that uses different methods than regular traceroute or tracert. For OS guessing more ports are better.

Exercises

5.27 Scan your own machine with nmap. Is the OS guessing valid?

5.28 Use the traceroute option on nmap using different ports:

```
nmap     -n    -Pn     --traceroute    --version-trace    -p80
hackerhighschool.org
```

5.29 Are there some differences on nmap traceroute using different ports and tracert or traceroute from your OS?

5.30 Research TCP/IP stack fingerprinting. How do you do it? Is it spoof-proof?

Using Scripts

Nmap also has a lot of useful scripts for scanning. You can use the `-script script-name` option to load scripts. One interesting script is `ipidseq`, which performs Incremental IP fingerprinting. This script can be used to find hosts for Idle Scan (-sI). This scan uses a problematic IP implementation on zombie hosts to scan other targets.

```
nmap --script ipidseq -oA hhs_5_ipidseq hackerhighschool.org

Starting Nmap 6.00 ( http://nmap.org ) at 2012-06-23 05:47 CEST
Nmap scan report for hackerhighschool.org (216.92.116.13)
Host is up (0.23s latency).
rDNS record for 216.92.116.13: isecom.org
Not shown: 971 closed ports
```

Exercises

5.31 Research Idle Scan techniques. What is it and how do you do it?

Conclusion to System Identification

Knowing where to look and what to look for is only part of the security battle. Networks are constantly being surveyed, analyzed, poked and prodded. If the network you are protecting isn't being watched then you aren't using the right tools to detect that behavior. If the network you're cracking isn't being watched, you may (may) get away with scanning it. As a cybersecurity expert, you should know every inch of the systems you are protecting – or testing. You need to know where the weaknesses are and where the strengths are as well, regardless of which side you're on.

Simply gathering up intelligence on a server, such as the operating system and open ports, isn't enough these days. An Advanced Persistent Threat will try to learn as much about your network as it can. This information includes -

- Firewall brand, model, firmware version, and software patches that exists

- Remote connections authentication, access privileges, and processes

- Other servers that connect to the network, this includes Email, HTML, back-up, redundant, off-site, hired or out-sourced services, and even contractors that may have used your network or are using it now

- Printers, fax machines, photocopiers, wireless routers, and network connections in your company waiting room

- Portable devices such as tablets, smartphones, digital picture frames, and anything that might connect to the network.

Even though we have covered many topics in this lesson, system identification covers an even broader area. There is quite a bit of information that flows through networks that identify parts of each device. Each device on the network can be exploited and thus used as an entry point for an attacker. Approaching this daunting challenge requires more than just software. Research your own equipment and learn as much as you can. That knowledge will pay off.

Alphabetical Index

NO WORRIES!
OSSTMMTRAINING.ORG

KNOWING HOW TO APPLY THE OSSTMM TAKES YOUR WORRIES AWAY.
OSSTMM TRAINING MAKES YOU A BETTER, MORE EFFICIENT SECURITY TESTER
AND ANALYST WHICH MAKES WHAT YOU NEED TO SECURE BE MORE SECURE.

ISEC⊙M

42331134R00081

Made in the USA
Middletown, DE
09 April 2017